I0486192

Monaco Experts Academy

written by

Zsolt Szemerszky

Monaco Experts Academy
- *written by Zsolt Szemerszky* -

First Printing: 2013

ISBN-13: 978-1519168573

ISBN-10: 1519168578

CreateSpace Independent Publishing Platform
Amazon.com

www.zsoltszemerszky.com

Dedication

Monaco Experts Academy is dedicated to people aiming to achieve their personal and business goals.

Our community shares the same goal of achieving visible results. No matter how the economic situation is there are always companies who are able to grown and to increase their wealth.

Monaco Experts Academy
- *written by Zsolt Szemerszky* -

Contents

Be in charge	15
Complaining	*15*
Tiger or Rabbit	*19*
The story of Peter	*24*
Basic Principles	27
Quality	*27*
Reaction	*29*
Increase	*31*
Complex thinking	*34*
Analysis paralysis	*36*
The right solution	39
Fresh views from outside	*39*
Don't change, just improve	*43*
Care of the industry sensitivity	*45*
Making a difference, being out of the box	*49*
Understanding your market	53
Understanding your market	*53*
Appropriate target groups	*56*
Creating Value	*61*
Positioning	*63*
Targeting your market	65
The key	*65*
Be an expert, show values	*66*

Targeting you competitors	*73*
The Trick	80
The three basic ingredients	*80*
Educate your target group	*83*
Five reasons why people do not buy from you (online)	*85*
Appropriate communication	*88*
Using formulas in the business life	*90*
AIDA formula	90
Best practices for Offer writing	91
CV formula	92
The weakness of the advertisement	*93*
Opt-In structure	*101*
Value page	102
Sequence page	105
Real-Estate vs. Wealth Management strategy	*107*
Step 1: Why will people interact with Barclays?	112
Step 2: Get the direct contact	113
Step 3: Qualify the prospects	115
The reverse side	*119*
Final thoughts	122

Monaco Experts Academy
- *written by Zsolt Szemerszky* -

Monaco Experts Academy
- written by Zsolt Szemerszky -

Introduction

Zsolt Szemerszky is a National Quality Prize Winner Revenue Specialist and Author.

His aim to help people and corporations to achieve their highest ambitions.

Being an author of multiple books, published in over 50 countries world-wide helped Zsolt Szemerszky to create business values for people and to motivate them in the road towards their aims.

One of Zsolt's most quoted sentence is:

> *"Every mountain can be climbed*
> *just you have to find the appropriate way to it.*
> *If somebody does not achieve it's goal*
> *then he has not done everything to achieve it.*
> *The secret of success is persistence!"*

As one of the top business crisis advisor, revenue specialist, performance and marketing expert, Zsolt's books, videos, newsletters and appearances now inspire millions of people worldwide.

Foreword

Capitalization of our personal and business potential highly depends on our willingness to learn and improve.

> *"You do not have to be Big to start, but you have to start to become Big!"* - Zig Zagler

This book has been created to all those people who have a strong desire to improve the quality of their life and their businesses.

This book is based on real life experiences and they ensure you the tools to control your future. **Give yourself a change to capitalize your own potentials!**

Important to mention that Monaco Experts Academy is free and independent from any kind of politics, religion, marketing agency, media, education organization, etc.. It is an independent business venture where we are committed to ensure you all the knowledge and ability to capitalize the maximum from your own potentials.

I hope that **my life experience will help you to achieve your highest ambitions!**

As the founder of Monaco Experts Academy personally, I spent 16 years in the business field as a company owner, revenue specialist and business process modeler. In 2006 I was honored with National Quality Prize and in 2008 I gained the Entrepreneur of the Year in SMB title. I am also proud that I am an Internationally published author as well with multiple books.

One of my most important lesson on my journey was that **those small things which makes the real difference can not be learn by school books**, only by life experiences. This is the reason why I am proud to ensure you my own life experiences as well.

Wishing you the very best of luck,

Sincerely,

Zsolt Szemerszky

Monaco Experts Academy
- written by Zsolt Szemerszky -

Monaco Experts Academy

written by

Zsolt Szemerszky

Monaco Experts Academy
- written by Zsolt Szemerszky -

Chapter 01
Be in charge

Complaining

There is one rule, maybe it is among the **most important rule**s. No matter what you are aiming to implement into your business or personal life **you have to be in charge!**

Many people are very passionate in the beginning but during the road when they continuously face obstacles this passion starts to fade. This is the point whereby they open the pipe for complaints.

Few years ago I noticed that in the modern society **it is usual to complain**. The first time I wrote about this in my book called "NO EXCUSE! in business".

I searched a lot for the reason and the source why we are not satisfied with our life. Finally I realized it. After I discovered the source of complaining my personal and business life started to improve. I got the chance to develop myself. It was really incredible because I realized that complaining is one of the **very first thing that we learn as infants**.

It is incredible how many business and life-coaching trainings are available, such as courses about improving your efficiency, your business performance or lectures about how you can be more balanced and happier in your personal life. This is why it was really strange that we can not really read about the source of complaining. Somehow people do not really talk about this. However complaining is all around us and I believe that the key to be happier is to **understand**

every little step of the road, which leads us towards our happiness.

Believe it or not complaining was among the very first things we have learnt as infants. This was a very easy method, which kept us alive.

People usually do things with reasons. Therefore you can also always find a reason why we are where we are in our business and/or our personal aims. Life is a big learning cycle where we all have the possibility to learn and to improve our skills. However as infants we made a **huge mistake** in our life. We misinterpreted some of the gestures, which started to **influence our whole life**.

As infants we learnt fast that if we are hungry then the only thing to do is to cry and our mother will run to us and feed us. We easily drew a lesson that crying equals with food. It was a very easy and clear message for us.

However we also learnt that when we are in pain, we can also use crying as a tool and our mother will run again to us, pick us up in her caring and loving arms to rock us to sleep.

Now this was a perfectly new thing, which meant that **crying equals with care and love**.

Our infantile brain put the picture together very fast and the result was simple: crying equals with love, care, food. Therefore crying became our Jolly Joker card. By time we noticed and understood that we are able to reach the **unconditional attention** of our parents simply by crying. And let's face it, this worked very well.

However what helped our survival in our very first years was a "**virus**", which **infected our future**. This was a "virus", which made us addictive and this still proliferates deep in our body.

So **we mixed up the attention with love** as the purpose of our own survival. But the two things are definitely not the same. This is the reason why many of us have never experienced real, true and unconditional love.

Usually I do not watch TV, but many years ago I had a favorite TV-series called Boston Legal. It was about an unusual friendship of two lawyers, maybe a friendship we are all looking for. Beside many of the inspiring thoughts I found one which made me really think during those times:

> *"People walk around today calling everyone their "Best Friend". The term doesn't have any real meaning any more. Mere acquaintances are lavished with hugs and kisses upon the 2nd or at most 3rd meeting... Birthday cards gets passed around in offices so everybody can scribble a snippet of sentimentality for a colleague that they've barely met. And everyone just loves everyone. As a result when you tell somebody you love them. Do they? I guess I'm not sure..."*
> - Boston Legal TV Series

Once I heard in a conference that we are living in an "**ego life**". The term ego life seems to be true because many of us love other people around us for what they can do for us and not for the fact who they really are.

So then why are we complaining?

Because we want attention!

People usually speak about their problems because they want attention. Attention, audition, understanding and absolution that everything will be fine and they did not do anything wrong.

However if we agree with the Law of Attraction, namely the name given to the belief that "like attracts like" and that by focusing on positive or negative thoughts, one can bring about positive or negative results, then we can easily state that by complaining we will attract only crap around us. When we are complaining then our brain and our spirit is focusing with full energy on the negative stuff, so let's put a bet on what life will bring us...

I can clearly state that there is nothing wrong with being afraid. In every situation when something happens differently from our plans we can easily loose our faith and we can go into hesitation. Even if it is hard to acknowledge for us during those times we all have fear in our heart.

We are all afraid from sudden changes, the new things and from the unknown. It is a natural human reaction. However it is not natural to focus on the problems instead of their **potential solutions**. When we were infants we had no other choice in our hands, but now as grownups the **decision is in our hands** and it is **only ours**.

Tiger or Rabbit

One of the most basic and important business rule is that **you are responsible for all your decisions, success or failures**. Only you!

However hard it is you can not blame the external factors. We are in the same business jungle and the rules are the same for all of us. No exceptions. It is all upon you if you will survive or not. It is all upon you if you will be a Rabbit or you will become a Tiger. Now days the business is your jungle, your playground.

If you do not like to be a Rabbit then change it. You are the master of your destiny. Do not blame others, that's the game of losers and cowards.

Never blame outside factors, never say what could be if... You need to **focus only on what you can do** now with all your assets. You need to bring out the best as much as possible from your current, existing knowledge, assets.

Economy, politics, weather, your neighbor, etc... it is easy to blame these factors for your failure, but believe it or not these factors influence also your competition not only you.

You can not change these factors, just as you can not change the politics. You need to accept them, acknowledge the rules and go forward towards your aims. Sitting and waiting for the changes is equal with suicide because you will lose the control over things.

One of my favorite example is coming from China. They really teach the freedom of choice, therefore in China **the word "crisis"** is written with **two symbols**.

The first symbol called "**Wei**" and it means "**crucial**" or "danger". In many times Wei is also referred to as "A time of danger".

Traditional symbol

Simplified symbol

The second symbol is called "**Gee**" which means "**opportunity**" or "A time of opportunity".

So in China the word crisis contains the "crucial" and the "opportunity" symbol as well. This is exactly the right philosophy of being a Tiger or a Rabbit in our life. As I used to call the angle of incidence of the Sun.

The decision is always yours!

From my personal point of view the one thing what I really hated in business is non-performance. Many people are lazy to do their homework or are simply just not ready to look around and to challenge their situations. However I have to admit that more than thirteen years ago I was the same too. I started to gain knowledge from the books, but when something happened which was not written in the books I started to panic.

After many years life crossed my roads with Dodo Newman, the Inspirationaliste and she taught me one very important thing, which was to **not give up our beliefs in a positive solution**. She taught me to keep up and to **continuously believe** in my aims.

> *"Passion cannot be learned, cannot be faked or copied. It is something that burns like fire, and if not kept alive, it soon can burn out.*
>
> *When I first meet people, often their first impression of me is that my philosophy and the way of thinking is far away from the standards, and sometimes they seem almost impossible.*
>
> *I believe that impossible means = i m possible."*
> - Dodo Newman

Most of us are ready to give up the fight without even realizing that maybe we are already in the finish line. Thanks to Dodo I realized that I can always challenge the existing because we are able to improve things, to innovate.

Since then I also know and this has become my philosophy, that **if you try something new you never lose, however you immediately lose when you give it up**.

You can do the same old methods hoping to survive or you can **take the opportunity and challenge** your market.

It is never easy as it seems but what is really easy is to wait and do nothing.

I was much younger when life dropped me serious challenges. I lost my mother when I was 23 and I also struggled to find new business channels. Those times one of my friend referred me a book which I highly recommend to everyone.

It is called "Who Moved My Cheese?" and the author is Dr. Spencer Johnson. It is a real bestselling title which has sold over 10 million copies worldwide. And the reason is quite obvious since the author found the language and tools to **deal with change**, an issue that makes all of us nervous and uncomfortable. Highly recommended reading.

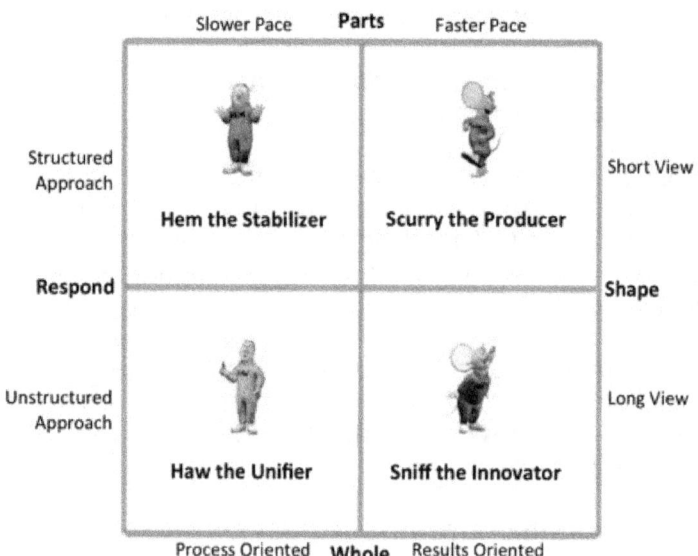

It is a book about four little mice. They are all looking for the cheese in a maze in a very changing and challenging time. The cheese represents their survival, cheese being a metaphor for what we want to have in life.

Sometimes we are all in a symbolical maze and **our survival highly depends on our decisions**, determination and the influence of the people around us.

The "Who Moved My Cheese?" is one of my favorite book, I read it many times and it's message is perfectly clear about one thing, the why and the when you should start to change.

And does it help in crisis, underperformance or any struggles in personal and business aims? I believe yes, because crisis could be your biggest opportunity!

So... **are you a Tiger or a Rabbit?**

The story of Peter

To be in charge is one of the most difficult thing in life. It is also hard because being charge means being responsible too.

When I was a kid I had a big lesson about decision and responsibilities. A very important lesson from life. It happened with me and my beloved mother Susan who passed away very early, she was only forty-two. I am know that she died without forgiven herself for the mistake she made. For me this was among my strongest life changing experiences which helped me to understand the difference between simple doing something or to be responsible for the outcome.

This story started very long time ago. I can hardly remember things, but this one thing is very clear in my mind. I was around eight years old, when we had a Christmas dinner. The whole family was together, the grandparents and the cousins as well. Around thirty people around the table. It was a beautiful pleasant night with full of love and laughter, until the point when something changed my life forever.

I was in the room of my cousin Peter. We played all night, but suddenly he hit me. I started to cry and scream loudly as I could so everybody run inside the room. The people around were shocked and they could not imagine what happened with me. Why this eight years old child cries with so much pain.

In that moment I fighter with my tears and I hardly breath and before I could tell what happened to me, my cousin Peter came up with an explanation. He told them that I became aggressive, beat him and he defended himself. It was a huge lie, but my mother came in the front and she gave me a big slap in my face.

I started to cry even harder and in the meantime Peter started to laugh. Nobody understood why he is so happy, but he just laughed further. When Peter's mother asked him, why is he laughing he said, because I did nothing, Peter just made it up. He confessed his lie and he was so happy that I got the slap meanwhile I did nothing wrong.

The next days my mother was very sad, she cried almost every day. One day, after hundreds of apologies she came to me again and she told me the this:

> *"Promise me Zsolt, that you will never let people mislead you. Sometimes we made our decision based on what we hear or see, but it could mislead us. We need to be more open to rethink what we see, hear, feel, we need to organise those data and we need to make a right decision. Immediate reactions could be fatal, we need to analyse and consider all the impressions we experience. I made a huge mistake that day my dear son, and please promise me that you will never made the same. And please also promise me that you will never let people to lie about you. Promise me to not let people to drop on you their cruelty or sadness."*

I promised her. But I knew that her heart was already broken because of her mistake. I was never angry to her about what happened, but for her it was hard to forgive to herself.

I do not know why but I still remember this story. This is still in my mind and I am sure that this will never go away. Maybe this is why I am alway insist to the right, to the truth.

However I also know that aiming to find out the truth is a good quality in any leader. Prejudice or half-information could lead us to wrong decision which can compromise our future success.

"The story of Peter" is always there for me to see both side of the coin before I make my decisions because real decisions always have consequences.

Chapter 02
Basic Principles

Quality

One of the most important **area for development** in any business is the quality. The word quality stands for many aspects such as effectiveness, efficiency, time, service, income, revenue, result, etc...

In this special case we are not talking about the technology, service or product behind Your Company, but the quality of effectiveness of the marketing.

The quality is among the most powerful things that any business entity can achieve because this will **make a difference** between Your Company and its competitors. Even if quality is not about selling and especially not income its result in terms of money will be seen immediately. With quickened work reactions, with more efficient business processes Your Company will **save time**, which will allow to have **more focus on development and innovation**.

The quality is the element that can make a bold difference for Your Company to stand out among its competitors. Based on my own experiences the current structure of many companies are not used to work in the time of challenges. Since 2008 the label of a product or company is simply not enough to gain remarkable results without the involvement of **new viewpoints** as well as new strategies. And with its new business development strategy Your Company have to face with **new competitors** in the foreign market.

Therefore when we are talking about quality we are also talking about the **mindset of our clients** and prospective clients.

Our number one aim with any business corporations is to **increase quality** in as many areas as we can cover. We will define all the aims and tasks, we will define their end-values as well as their weight related to its success of that field. By having a weighted point system we will be able to create a measurement strategy, which will lead us to various statistics.

By using weekly, monthly and yearly **statistics** and **executive dashboards** we will able to immediately see the critical points and we will have the tool to react.

The aim is to deliver drill-down dashboards which are more than just raising attention to the problem or the areas where Your Company should strengthen its market position. The drill-down dashboard technology helps us to find out the **real source of the problems**, therefore we will be able to solve the problem and protect Your Company from any similar future problems. Another advantage of the dashboard driven systems is that they **fasten up** the decision making processes because it is possible to see immediately the major differences based on the pre-defined alerts.

By improving the **measurement system**, we will immediately improve the quality since we will allow no space for errors. It will also motivate the employees to work faster and get the jobs done in a higher quality.

Reaction

One of the biggest disadvantage of a company is when its **reaction** is **too slow** to the market needs. And this can be especially true when Your Company is aiming to enter to a foreign market.

The times have changed and the economic spectrum has changed as well. By involving the **Internet**, **technology** into any business decision process the quantity of information has exploded and the **decision making** times have been **reduced**.

Now in the time of online communication the prospective clients easily "**shop**" around on the Internet reducing their time and expanding their opportunities. They have the possibility to overview ten companies in half an hour. So Your Company needs to deliver the requested and often client, region and service specific solutions in a **custom tailored way**.

We are in a time where **competition** dangers the traditional values. Anyone has the power to set-up a catchy business website and to spread out a message, which can compete the traditions and the many years of experience which Your Company delivers. Therefore the **timeframe** of reaction in communication became a very important **key issue**.

Also this is the reason why many companies have already **disadvantages** in foreign markets because they are unable to realize the **marketing gaps** and the new markets around themselves. This way they become second and third and their competitors will be remembered as leaders in those fields.

The most important thing is to realize that we are living in the age of technology, therefore we have to utilize the **advantages of technology** to gain better **communication**, faster **decisions** and **reactions** from our prospective clients.

Increase

To **include the local specialities, characteristics** within the Global strategy is among the key issues for the increase of the client base of Your Company. In many cases the standard ready-made approach cannot be used, Your Company needs **custom tailored** strategy focusing on the specific needs of its widely diversified target group.

Unfortunately daily-routine driven people can easily loose their creativity and lack of imagination causing difficulties in opening new business channels. This is why outside views and fresh ides can refresh the creativity.

Most of the company leaders are afraid from the marketing and PR areas because they have had bad experiences. In the last 10 years most companies focused only on buying advertisements, organizing various networking events without generating major results.

In life one of the most important thing is **communication** as You probably also know this. Communication, which should always be **two ways**. Marketing is about more than events and PR is about more than press releases and advertisements.

The main task in any marketing strategy is to **generate reaction**. The end result with all activities and strategies is not the event, the press release or the article in itself but is to **achieve overall reaction**. And this specific case we need to reach global overall reaction for Your Company.

Most of the big corporations measure marketing activities by the number of the events or the media appearances. Most marketing experts forget that the main aim is to generate result and not the amount of press releases and advertisement. It is clear to state that any event or advertisement, which is not generating direct result is a waste of time, money and energy.

To increase the client base of Your Company we need to make a difference, we have to **stand out from the crowd** and we have to communicate this **message** to a well **selected target group**, instead of focusing on the mass. Not everyone is able to relocate or not everyone is smart enough to diversified its company, therefore we are not targeting all the people in Europe, we are targeting a selected group of qualified prospects.

We have to admit that in the foreign market there is a new and highly competitive market for Your Company with multiple providers. In many cases the clients are shopping around just to get an impression, weight their decisions and in many cases some free gifts. These activities of shopping around often lead to these clients choosing a competitor.

This can be very annoying, however it does not mean that Your Company can not offer better or higher quality it only means that Your Company is unable to capitalize its potential at the moment. This is like "flirting" because the prospective clients are trying to find the "best looking" competitors therefore the prospective client will continuously **compare**.

To protect Your Company from the trap of being compared we need to **stand out** from the crowd, this way we also **protect ourselves** from the force of the competition.

For example in the Mobile sector usually a Telecommunication service is based on the **solution** what it can provide. Let the "apples" compete with each other. If Your Company is the only "pear" then it does not need to compete anymore because the prospective clients **can not compare** its added values to the **mass**.

The key word: **DIFFERENCE**!

Complex thinking

NO! **We do not want complexity!** We want to make everything more clear and more understandable.

People like to see things **complicated**. This is specially true with big corporate giants. Working for world leading corporations such as Alstom Power, IBM, BOLS, Carrefour, etc. I always experienced that employees live in a mystery. Sometimes the corporate **processes** are way **too complicated** and this can create a **confusion** and a **lack of efficiency** from the side of the employees.

During my past professional work experiences I have spent many weeks **interviewing** all the involved people, decision leaders in the business processes, our aim was to understand and optimize them to **avoid** such **outcomes** as this picture below depicts.

What I have learnt during the last 15 years is that **complex thinking makes people less effective** in their fields of activity. Less efficiency can lead to **lack of imagination**, which stops our chances to open new business channels when they are really necessary.

To develop, gain result and quality in any business sector the most important thing is to create **simple** and well **connected** business **processes** that employees relate to in a clear way. This gives a transparent overview to all the involved parties and a much better understanding.

When people fully understand the corporate processes **they are ready to come up with innovative ideas**. Usually we can notice that **people** who are **afraid** to make **suggestions** in business areas **do not fully understand** what is really going on in their own business areas.

Any kind of **improvement** comes from **fully understanding** the specific area and by making it as **transparent** and **clear** as possible to the people working within it.

Analysis paralysis

If you understand, acknowledge and agree with all the above mentioned obstacles named as Quality, Reaction, Increase and Complex thinking, then you will agree that some positive and innovative changes are necessary. However I have to admit, and this is my experience as well that **change is one of the most feared thing after death**.

> *"If you want to make a permanent change, stop focusing on the size of your problems and start focusing on the size of you!"* - T. Harv Eker

People like the balance and the regularity in their life, therefore changes are often considered as something negative. However changes are never bad, because by changing and challenging the existing we have a very good position to improve our skills and our business.

I would like to highlight that you can not achieve anything without contrast and fear, but what is fear? T. Harv Eker wrote once that FEAR is False Evidence Appearing Real.

The thing is that people who are unable to decide and go for the positive changes often fall into the **side effect of fear**, which is **analysis paralysis**.

In 2005 Malcolm Gladwell published a book called "Blink: The Power of Thinking Without Thinking". It presents in popular science format research from psychology and behavioral economics on the adaptive unconscious; mental processes that work rapidly and automatically from relatively little information. It considers both the strengths of the adaptive unconscious, for example in expert judgment, and its pitfalls such as stereotypes.

The author describes the main subject of his book as "thin-slicing": our ability to gauge what is really important from a very narrow period of experience. In other words, this is an idea that spontaneous decisions are often as good as —or even better than— carefully planned and considered ones. Gladwell draws on examples from science, advertising, sales, medicine, and popular music to reinforce his ideas. Gladwell also uses many examples of regular people's experiences with "thin-slicing."

Gladwell explains how an expert's ability to "thin slice" can be corrupted by their likes and dislikes, prejudices and stereotypes (even unconscious ones), and how **they can be overloaded by too much information**.

We do that by "thin-slicing," using limited information to come to our conclusion. In what Gladwell contends is an **age of information overload**, he finds that experts often make **better decisions with snap judgments** than they do with volumes of analysis.

Gladwell gives a wide range of examples of thin-slicing. Gladwell also mentions that sometimes having too much information can interfere with the accuracy of a judgment, or a doctor's diagnosis.

> *"Analysis paralysis: sometimes having too much information can interfere with the accuracy of a judgment."* - Malcolm Gladwell

This is commonly called "**Analysis paralysis**". The challenge is to sift through and **focus on only the most critical information to make a decision**. The other information may be irrelevant and confusing to the decision maker. Collecting more and more information, in most cases, just reinforces our judgment but does not help to make it more accurate.

The collection of information is commonly interpreted as confirming a person's initial belief or bias. Gladwell explains that better judgments can be executed from simplicity and frugality of information, rather than the more common belief that greater information about a patient is proportional to an improved diagnosis. **If the big picture is clear enough to decide, then decide from the big picture without using a magnifying glass.**

The conclusion is that if you feel that something could improve your qualities, go for it immediately before someone else will utilize it. Be a leader and do not make the mistake to fall into the follower category, simply just because you can not see the material way. Our inside always guide us to the right way.

Chapter 03
The right solution

Fresh views from outside

It is a fact that most people are unable to get an unbiased, objective view of problems from inside. Therefore if Your Company is aiming to improve its quality, result and its corporate efficiency it is always good to have a fresh new thinking from a person who knows the **LOCAL NEEDS**, as well who knows, understands and is able to challenge the existing business processes to compete against the competitors from the global market.

An improvement such as the offered co-operation goes well beyond what Your Company is used to be doing in the traditional ways. Once the aimed results in the pilot location are achieved all the gained results and best practices will be available to be extended and to be implemented globally all around your target countries. This way Your Company will have a well structured and tested know-how to achieve more clients, more revenue and to improve quality, which will advance the corporate culture as well.

I would like to summarize for you the **benefits** and the **clean results** what you will implement after reading this book at Your Company. I believe we both want to see exceptional **results in a very short term**.

You will have **new prospective clients,** and I will **optimize** and **challenge** many of **your market approach business processes**, which are related to marketing, sales, and PR. This way you will have actual tools to **measure** them, which will ensure you the possibility to **improve** their **quality** and you will have a **clear view** about the **expenses**, which have and have no return.

When I am talking about return I am always making a difference between **clean return** (in house efficiency) and **targeted return**.

By talking about clean return I mean returns, which are **independent** from the economic situation, therefore improving them you will have more **time for innovation** and of course this extra time already means a result, which you can **measure in terms of money. By optimizing some processes you will have more work done for the same amount of salary.**

By **improving and optimizing** your new client related processes (such as marketing, sales, pr, client reps, etc...) we can increase the productivity and this would mean for Your Company **extra budget for further developments**.

Based on my professional experiences in world leading companies I will provide you the know-how, which will give you the possibility to change and replace the old and non-working processes.

I believe that most of the companies has a much bigger, international market. In other hand by focusing only on local events, **Your Company IS CLOSING ITS DOORS** in front of the global prospects.

The local activities are NECESSARY, however they are ONLY complimentary tools for a bigger marketing strategy, which focuses on the new and prospective clients. The main aim is to bring new clients to Your Company, which allows to **capitalize its potentials** and to **improve its quality**.

The most important with the marketing strategies is to reach any kind of **REACTION**. If they are unable to gain reactions then money spent on them is wasted. This is why I do not prefer the traditional advertisements, because they are not direct and cannot be measured.

Out of the Box marketing involves low or **zero budget ideas** because the focus is on the result with unique concepts, since success lies in the **strategic idea combined with efficient implementation. 99% of opportunities are lost by wrong and bad implementation, these are the cases when the excuse becomes the idea**.

Our main aim have to improve Your Company in many fields, with exceptional tools which allows to **capitalize our potential** by creating **integrated marketing channels**.

This way we can also **measure efficiency** through executive **dashboards** and it gives us the possibility to **change** and **reorganize** campaigns in **real time**, which usually can not be done with traditional marketing strategies.

I believe that this type of **operational advantage**, thinking in target groups and specific processes through our marketing strategy brings the advantage to be the "Nice and juicy Green Pear", which **stands out** from all the other "boring rad apple" ones. Plus by having the right measuring tools we can **continuously improve** our skills.

I also think that Your Company needs to **make a difference** and it has all the potential to achieve it, however currently Your Company is **unable to**

capitalize it. This is why Your Company needs a **fresh and outstanding view**.

Furthermore the marketing should be built up based on **pure results**. It is easy to ask for a new and increased budget, however **if result cannot be gained from a small budget then what kind of result can be expected from an increased budget?**

Your Company's main aim should be an **increased client base**, full of new and **super satisfied clients**. This is the base for the future developments.

Since marketing is much more than holding events (monitoring the competitors, analyzing the market, trends, building up continuously good relations with the current clients, campaign planning, monitoring, statistics, etc...) I will be ready to guide you to **implement all the strategies** I deliver to Your Company.

EXECUTIVE = latin Executor

ex: fully
sequi: monitored

I want to execute the potentials of Your Company, because **I want to see the results at the end**. By the end of these chapters I will aim to deliver new clients for Your Company and I will also deliver very clean statistics, measuring tools which **avoid any excuse**.

Don't change, just improve

I believe that the current marketing of Your Company is very important.

However what I am offering is a very **different type of philosophy** where we will be able to **improve** the current marketing approach and we can **deliver** results in terms of new and super satisfied clients.

Earlier this year I saw a very nice picture from the French artist Cote, which clearly shows how market has changed (in a funny way...). I believe that our number one aim with Your Company is to keep the fish in the foreign market instead of competing with them.

My experience, as an entrepreneur and business owner is to focus on new clients, target groups especially when it comes to out of the box cases with the **result of visible growth**. Therefore my aim is **not to interfere** with Your Company's **current marketing methods** because what I am offering is something way more different in terms of solutions and results.

1913

2013

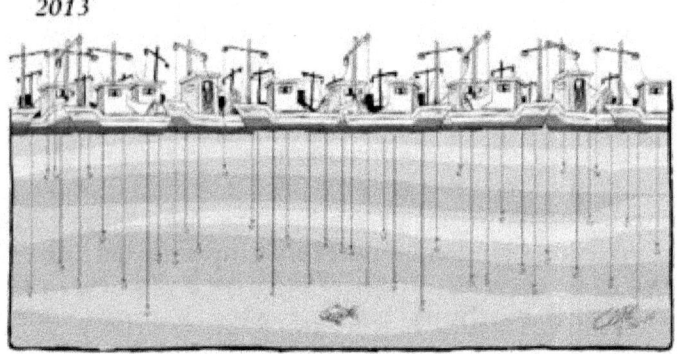

Care of the industry sensitivity

In general we can state that many business segment is among the most conservative and traditional segments in the World (such as bank and wealth management industry). Therefore many marketing experts believe it offers a limited field for creativity because they can not involve new items.

Thinking and creating in an out of the box way does not mean that one has to go the extreme, away from values, traditions. **Making a difference doesn't mean we have to move away from traditions, history, values or that we have to be shocking.**

To think outside the box is **trying not to think of the obvious things**, but trying to **think beyond them** and so bringing in something new, something unique. However a change is necessary in the general approach in order to create something different.

> "*You can not make anything different by doing the same things continuously, you can not expect to achieve your aims which is something new, by doing the same things in the same way with the same tools, with the same people in the same environment.*" - Dodo Newman

The thing is that marketing is all about creativity, therefore real creative people can deliver out of the box solutions to improve our productivity and our results. And this is the point where I would like to highlight that **result means improvement and new income**.

I had to think about the way to explain this to you in written then suddenly I remembered one of my favorite sushi bar in Berlin, Germany. As you know coming from a different country and experiencing many cultural environments people always see interesting or unique ideas. For me one of these ideas was found in a tiny sushi bar in Berlin.

So to present the **Out of the Box marketing philosophy** I would like to introduce the example of "rice pipes":

The "rice pipes" experience is based on the traditional sushi recipes, however the end product makes a horizontal effect instead of the traditional vertical one, plus the "rice pipes" are twice as long as the traditional sushi.

The reason why I present this example here is because what the "rice pipes" concept does is to **use all the existing without implementing any new material**. The **key ingredient is the creativity**, which makes the whole concept **sell**.

> **Rice pipes:**
> ★ Nothing changed compared to sushi
> ★ No new ingredients involved

However concepts such as "rice pipes" are much more than this. Let's imagine that Your Company has a very **conservative base** and a very sensitive market in Europe. They like the existing and definitely traditional ways of approach. Let's call them the sushi lovers. For them **we will offer the same and existing approaches and strategies** to make them satisfied.

But we can approach a **brand new target group** as well by introducing the **fresh concept**, which in this example is the "rice pipes". Did we really change our services or products? No. We just **diversified them** based on the market needs. And at the end of the day it is all about to realize the **market gaps** and to **be the first** who is able offer them the **solution**.

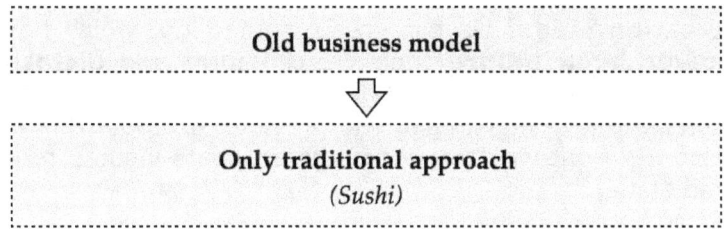

In the example above we can offer traditional approach (sushi) and out of the box approaches ("rice pipes").

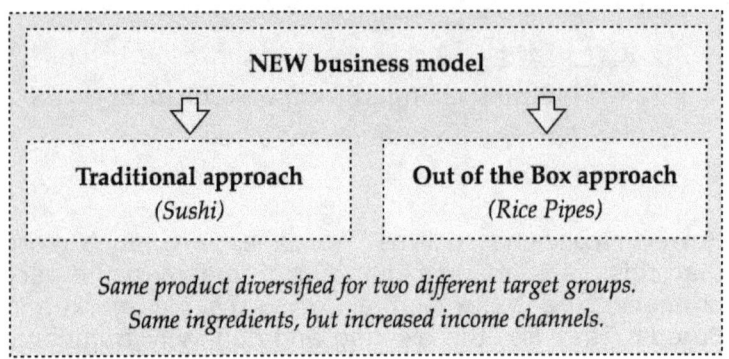

The approach for the diversified target market of Your Company should be based on the same out of the box principles. Your Company has everything it need we just need to find the way to present it to the various targets.

The conclusion is simple **we do not need to change the service and financial standards to create out of the box innovation**. All we need to do is to **collect** all the **possibilities** (ingredients) offered and allowed by the industry and to **mix them into a new creation**. And if we can create something, which has **never been before** then we can form and **dictate** that market without having to compete with the competitors. Referring to the previous example this is also the right way to become green pears instead of a red apple.

Making a difference, being out of the box

The main aim of any marketing strategy is to make a bold difference in the fields of Your Company. Therefore we need to focus on **result oriented solutions**, which will deliver the necessary improvement. To achieve positive and remarkable results we need to **focus on being out of the box** instead of **making similar activities** as all our competitors.

Earlier this year I created a visual for one of the Wealth companies here in the Principality of Monaco, Barclays.

I decided to show you exactly the same example. It will be a wealth management related example however you can interpret it to your foreign market as well.

When we are talking about private banking or private wealth management in Monaco the choices are **concentrated** in a very small place. Even if we are able to make a difference in any field, Monaco still offers many alternative solutions for the Investor. This is the reason why targeting new clients is very challenging.

This is why we need to make a difference. **People need a difference to make their choices!**

Below I **visualize** something from an outside point of **view of a foreign client**, which I call a little "Barclays game".

Choosing a bank is an easy issue compared to choosing a wealth management company. Can we find in the below picture the two "BAR" symbols one standing for Barclays Wealth Asset Management and the other for Barclays Wealth?

Monaco Experts Academy
- written by Zsolt Szemerszky -

```
B J S L C L B P M B P O B N P B S I
C A I C I C C D N C F M C M U C S U
E F G H S B K B L M M S S G B S G E
A W M A N D A P E A A C A J H A M A
B A R A S S A V A B P S B A S B J B
R O T B H A B M M B P A B E D B N P
B S I C A I C A R C R E C E B C G M
C C S C I T C P O C M B C M G C C M
C F F C F M C M M E R C E I M E U R
E U C F I S G G P G O S G R M B A R
2 P M G S J J U P K B L K V A L B P
L L B M L S M M S M A M M G F M V P
M C S M F I M A S M G S M L G O M D
P A M P R O S A M S A T S E C S F E
S L C S P P S G B S M C S G A S J P
T D C T H Y C F M B N P U B S R O T
```

The Answer:

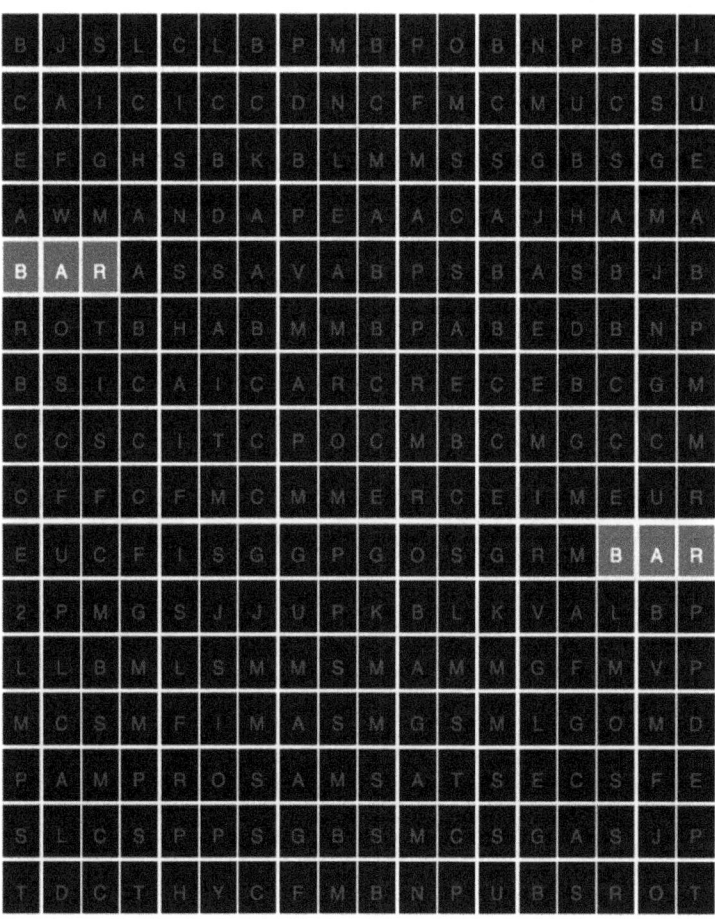

The only thing that I wanted to show with these game examples is that everyone working at Your Company clearly know how good Your Company is since they are **insiders**, however in a foreign and highly competitive market a prospective client who is an **outsider** sees many alternative choices, **continuously comparing, shopping around**.

It is quite clear that the competition is high.

Conclusion: any businesses or companies new market **expansion can be challenged only through change**.

I know people are afraid of changes, however **changes** are always **good** and **innovative** as well. The competitors are continuously looking for new ways, continuously changing. Your Company should not follow them, should not be the second or third company on the market, it should overtake them and be allowed to grow and develop.

I always considered myself as a very out of the box person and I **never give up on the obstacles** for an aim. I developed this skill during the past years, because all the projects I worked on needed very out of the box views to **gain the necessary results**.

My philosophy is:

Do not fear change,

FEAR FROM YOUR COMPETITORS!

Chapter 04
Understanding your market

Understanding your market

The human nature have a big problem related to confidence. It is very hard to say for us that we do not understand something. We are in a society where everybody is "forced" to know everything, to be involved in various activities and to be expert in its field.

During the first meeting almost 100% of my clients state that they understand their field of business, the need of their customers as well as their market. However the truth is that even if you know your market area well, **the market is in a continuous change**. Just imagine how was the economic in 2006, in 2010 and how it is now. To give you an example I share with you my own experience in the Principality of Monaco.

In 2010 when I arrived to Monaco I decided to change the market and I was ready to create something great to support the local businesses and by this act to gain some trust.

So I created a news and information aggregator portal called MonacoWealthManagement.com which targeted my potential clients.

I pushed very had this service but somehow **it did not really performed** as I imagined. I also received a letter from Mr. Michel Roger the Minister of State of Monaco that my activity does not seems professional.

I was really mad because I was **in the belief** that my service is excellent and I ensure the highest quality. In my mind my business model was perfect. And this was the **number one reason** for my temporary **failure**, my **ego**.

When you are not open to understand your market you will have a strong chance to fail. I had sixteen years of business experience with Fortune companies in various countries, I got National Quality Prize and I was the Entrepreneur of the Year, therefore I already decided what Monaco needs. I was so wrong.

Every market is different and every business sectors and countries have their own specialities. This is a learning cycle, where we can build up things based on our experience and knowledge, but **we can not leave out the specific views** from the execution of our visions.

In order to ensure you a short and little example let me highlight the MonacoWealthManagement.com portal which had a section specially dedicated for Lawyers. I collected and listed all the Lawyers and Financial advisors I found and I listed them under the section of Lawyers and Legal advisors. I knew that there are some differences such as "Avocats-Défenseur" or "Avocat", but I was sure that Avocats-Défenseur stands for defines lawyers meanwhile Avocat is a general lawyer.

As we all know in many cases **success relies only in one tiny thing**. For me this was the meaning of the words. In Monaco there is a huge different between these words. When you finish the law school you start as Avocats-Stragiaire for three years, after that for the next five years you are Avocat. So basically you will be a full powered lawyer, called Avocats-Défenseur only after eight years. Therefore when I listed the "juniors" with the "masters" they were not happy and they refused all the co-operation. Not to mentioned that many of them criticised that the Legal advisors are not even approved by the Monaco BAR.

The realisation of this little misunderstanding with the words took me two years. If was a big struggle for me however the solution was very easy. Since then I created different sections and now everybody is happy, the business prospers.

What I would like to share with my example is that **understanding your market is considered among the number one priorities in any businesses**. One little misunderstanding, one tiny details, one wrong approach can destroy your business. Meanwhile if you are patient enough to take the energy to understand your market then you can capitalise all of its potential. Therefore you are ready to **be in charge** of your future and you are ready to make **significant steps** to achieve your aims.

Appropriate target groups

I would like to highlight that *(in addition to entertainment and electronics,)* marketing is the world's second fastest-growing business.

It is especially interesting that **70% of people** working in the marketing segment **do not know** what marketing is. It is almost a trend of today that everyone is competent in everything so that **specialization has disappeared**.

Real marketing is to **catch the attention of your well-defined target group**.

The target group is the minority who is interested in your offer and who interests you as well. Naturally you can have more target groups as well.

One of my first observation was during my last years in business that most of the companies have very widely diversified target groups. Therefore for us the number one task of marketing is **defining the target group** and the **building of confidence.**

Usually when we start to build up a business growth plan most of the company owners and leaders are confident in their target groups and the answer is almost always the same:

- ➡ Individuals
- ➡ Business corporations
- ➡ Local individuals
- ➡ Local businesses
- ➡ Foreign individuals
- ➡ Foreign businesses

Furthermore (and unfortunately I rarely hear this):

➡ Small business

➡ SMB

➡ Corporate giants

➡ etc...

What is always very important is to drill down the categories. You have to think about each target groups sector specifically as well.

For example if you are a Telecommunication service provider:

➡ Business entities

    ➡ Foreign market

    ➡ Corporate giants

        ➡ IT providers

            ➡ Pharmacy

            ➡ FMCG

            ➡ Tobacco

            ➡ Retail & Logistics

            ➡ Financial (Bank, Wealth manager & Traders)

        ➡ etc...

As you can see each **business segment needs different types of business solutions**. One of them will look for Cloud service, another one for iPad integration with the central database (For example: FMCG representatives), another one for data migration services, in the Finance sector they are looking for fast information approach, etc...

You as a Telecommunication company (in this example) are able provide solution for each requirements for sure. However if you target them with the wrong solution then you make the **wrong approach** which **can lead you to loose** the Prospective **Client**.

Wrong approach:

When you approach a Bank with Cloud service they will probable refuse you immediately. The basic reasons: the liability of data storage on the Internet and/or the risk of having internal and confidential information in a public platform (security concerns).

Right approach:

One of the right approach could be offering them fast Internet channels with <u>information aggregator</u>. When you are able to provide information faster than your competitors than it is a multi-million Euro advantage in the trading business. It is a market gap! This is a solution which would interest them.

Of course we can separate the target groups in many business sectors from micro sized to corporate giants.

A perfect micro sized business could be found in the real-estate sector. In many cases the real-estate companies are working with less than 5 employees and usually with only one office. However they also have a very diversified target group and I believe it is key importance for them to understand the needs what they have to serve.

Or if you are in the Real-Estate business (in Monaco for example):

➡ Private individuals

   ➡ Foreign individuals

      ➡ Investment purpose

      ➡ Relocation

      ➡ Residency

      ➡ Prestige

      ➡ Retirement

      ➡ Heritage planning

      ➡ Business

      ➡ Mixed usage (Private & Business from the same apartment)

      ➡ etc...

And so on... There are many reasons why people are looking for a service or a product.

It is not enough to just define your target group because without marketing you will loose your target group. This is the tricky part... **Marketing generates people** who are interested in your product or solution (and the **sales** people **will close** the deal).

Trust is particularly important in the case of marketing, we call this **credibility**. This can help to measure that if we say something **how our target group will agree on it** and receive it. **Trust must be earned!**

If you already have a target group who trusts you, you can gain a **significant advantage** during every marketing campaign.

Creating Value

Creating value in simple terms means creating products or **services that people WANT**!

It is very important to remember that <u>everyone can see the price</u> of the product but not its value! We need to show and **teach the value** of the product in all cases. The real power lies in the value, which is represented by your products or solutions.

However without understanding your business territory, your market and your target groups you will perhaps survive but you will never prosper in the way you could.

The aim is generating revenue and profit, therefore you need to clearly understand what are the needs of your market, target group. You need to know what they are looking for, what is their decision criteria, etc...

There is a bad news for you...
There are different types of buyers:

➡ some of them are only looking at the price

➡ some of them are looking for the best quality

➡ some of them are looking for the prestige

➡ some of them are looking for long term guarantees

➡ some of them are looking for the added values

➡ some of them simply make their decisions based on your personality

➡ etc...

Many-many different needs but you need to know and handle them.

The price is only one factor and believe it or not, the **price is not the most important one**. If you will start to <u>fight on the price you will die</u>.

Many companies have no other idea how to communicate with their target group so they simply reduce the price. But this is just a silent and desperate scream for new customers, clients. If you understand the needs of your clients you do not need to reduce the price anymore. You will have the possibility to sell for a higher price than your competition without risking to loose your clients.

The most efficient way towards achieving business success is to understand the needs of your target group. This way you will be able to build **campaigns** to gain **benefits from the individual perspectives**.

Positioning

When you understood your market and you have a good insight what your prospective clients want then **you need to start to position** yourself.

The history of positioning goes back to the 1970s, it is possible to find a lot of ways since then how it has been used. But what does the word "positioning" mean? I try to demonstrate it to you with a few questions:

1., Who was the first man on the Moon?
Ok. Maybe it is easy, but who was the second? Do you know? No?! No problem, let's go forward...

2., Who was the first person who flew over the Atlantic Ocean?
Let me help you: Charles Lindbergh. And who was the second? Do you know? No?! No problem, let's go forward...

3., What is the highest mountain in the World?
Mount Everest. And the second one? Etc...

I hope you understand now the real meaning of positioning. **People usually remember only the best**, the first One. If you want to be successful in your PR, **you have to place your product or solution to the first place in the mind of your target group**.

If your product is not in the first place, you will loose a big potential market.

Never focus on the money, because the real power lies in the value, which is represented by your products or solutions. If you have learned to create value, then you still have further tasks since you need to sell your products or solutions.

If your PR is successful, then you have created value for your target group, that is you have well-positioned your product or solution. The next task for marketing is to look for your potential buyers, customers, who want your products, services. The sales performs the closing process, it makes it possible for your customers to buy from You.

The PR, marketing and sales functions should never be mixed up. Although one does not exist without the other, it is necessary to separate them and to know which is responsible for what, what is the end result we expect from each of them.

People want a product that has had a good PR, so it's easy to find out its potential circle of customers, the sales is just one simple step after this. Many companies, businesses commit an error that they only focus on the sales, while it carries out the least work within the work process. The actual work begins in the reverse way.

Chapter 05
Targeting your market

The key

During my professional career I attracted the idea takers like a magnet. I believe it is the part of any business life. Many people believes that the idea itself can earn them the big return. In the real life the idea worth nothing without proper execution. **The key is always found in the implementation process.**

In very rare cases you can go forward only with an idea, but mainly the success comes when you can **combine the idea, with the life experience and the passion**.

I always like to work with the people who originated a concept, a vision or idea. They are the ones who are ready to fight for it, they are the creators of the vision and usually the most passionate supporters during the execution process.

The value of an idea is always reflects in the execution methods. When people unable to capitalise an idea that can lead back to two reason:

- ➡ lack of information about the market
- ➡ wrong implementation

In any good business model ideas, **visions and implementation could go hand in hand**. They should support each other to fulfill the final and higher goal.

Be an expert, show values

As we always say it is not enough to know a service or a product but you have to present proudly your knowledge to your target group. **Creating value in simple terms means creating products or services that people WANT!**

Some years ago a huge new market has opened to us through the Internet. We overcame the invincible and were able to communicate our products to places which were unimaginable before. **Distances disappeared** and suddenly huge choices of products appeared. It became increasingly easier to make business, particularly in the area of trade and by now anyone can start their own web shop in almost an hour.

New opportunities have also opened up for cheaters, and the previous confidence has turned over to mistrust. The new technologies unfortunately bring with themselves new abuses. Because of the daily scam letters or the time wasters, who want nothing more than to collect ideas, to benchmark, serious suspicions arose that has set back the intentions of the customers as well. Therefore, **it is not enough if the product is just good**.

The value has always been a relative concept, which is based on the personal judgement of the customer. The real product has never an absolute value, a product is worth as much as the buyer is willing to pay for it in exchange. All you need to achieve for this is for the customer to want the product.

The customer is capable to do only one thing, to bargain excellently. This is what the business life has taught the customer. If the same product is sold in more places, the customer will buy it where it is the cheapest. If you want to avoid that customers compare your prices, then show them that there are other considerations, criteria as well. This is what we call customer teaching or client education. The aim is **to show our customers that what they are buying is not a price tag**, it is much more than that.

It is very important to remember that everyone can see the price of the product but not its value! We need to show and teach the value of the product in all cases.

The best is if we are able to add a plus to the product, which makes it unique, makes it more than its competitors and we offer them to those who have needs for exactly these pluses, who want exactly these products with their added values.

Anything can be sold to someone if he wants it even though he does not need it, but nothing can be sold that he does not want even if he needs it. The key is to find out what your client wants and to serve this need, since the value is no other than the fact of how much they want your product.

It is worth asking your customers what they want, what is most needed, what problems they face, then look at how your services, products help them and put the emphasis onto the problems, so that your customers see that they need this product, that they WANT it. If you do this well, then you have also almost positioned your product.

Let me share with you another example for Monaco which is happening here during the last years.

The Principality of Monaco offers exceptional possibilities for Investors and Wealthy individuals. If you are wise enough you can find experts who are able to offer you diversified solutions to protect and increase your wealth.

However in the land of glamour and wealth, people (let's be correct, some of the people) realised the wind of change and they grabbed this opportunity. It was great to experience during the past years that the advisors started to really focus on the personal needs as well and they took care about the custom tailored solutions.

For an experienced HNWI investor trust is a very key issue, specially with high level investments. Many people tend to make the mistake of judging projects based on the promised profit and income, and other so-called material factors behind them. However the real value is not the promise, the real value at the end of the day is the result.

The past years of economic situation clearly showed that the numbers and indicators are not enough anymore for the HNWI investors to invest. The HNWI **investors are becoming more educated and informed** because of their loss during the economic crisis, and the personal trust in the wealth managers has become first priority. They more and more shy away from big institutions, because of their negative experiences with their **sales driven representatives** and their bonus oriented account officers. That's why they are looking for a fair and sometimes independent partners who is in place for a lifetime, who strives to achieve the client's **"peace of mind" feeling**, the match of personality and portfolio.

I consider this as one of the reason why there are many new Family Offices, because they have realised a market gap. At some point of the business development we need to open to new markets as well. There is one point in the life cycle of all business where by focusing on local businesses there are no further possibilities.

I believe that after the economic crisis most of the HNWI investors are looking for long term partners. **Only those companies perform in the long term, which are not hunting for fast profit but gaining results with secured investments to show their client base their competency. The HNWI investors are keen to find partners who they trust, trust which his not entirely based on pure numbers.** HNWI investors are continuously looking for result oriented, sharp minded wealth managers and investment advisors.

Last year when I talked with one of my investor friend he summarised really well the needs. **HNWI investors are not looking for high return, they simply do not want to loose.** They are also satisfied with small growth, but they hate to loose. The focus of the HNWI investors has changed.

Before 2008 every wealth manager and advisor used a process to approach, which builds up a value for their wealth services. This converts a potentially valuable wealth management solution into a really valuable one. When we know that if a client really wants something then price does not really matter anymore. Because price is easy, everybody knows that 7% interest rate is less than 12% interest rate. However after 2008 trust has become number one priority. Everybody sees the promises, but the wealth advisors in Monaco had to show the HNWI investors their values as well.

Let's see everything with the eye of an investor. Let's say that we have two trees, which are representing two wealth management companies. Both trees have the similar size of crown but their trunks are different in size. Because of the difference of the trunk size they have different types of roots as well. In the picture the HNWI investor is standing between the two trees.

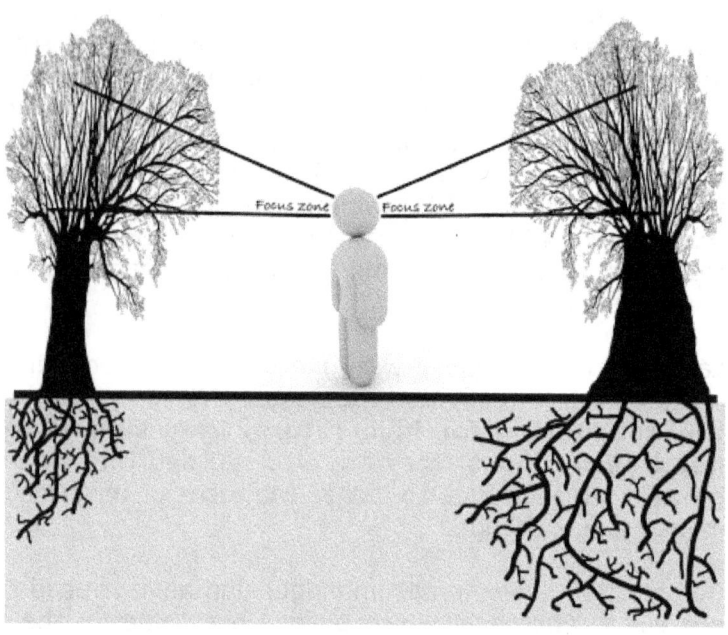

In a calm economic situation and without being educated this is how clients see the companies. The trees are the companies and usually everybody is looking at the tree crown, which is the biggest visible surface. Let's say it is the packaging of the tree, therefore all marketing, pr and sales experts are aiming to present it in the most delicate and fancy way.

When you are focusing only on the profit then you can easily be misled by the illusion of the crown. This is among the major reason why so many investors have lost their funds all around the World. We have to accept that many banks around the Globe focus on the brand message instead of the intense growth of new clients. Maybe this was the biggest lesson to learn during the economic crisis. So let's **change the focus** of the HNWI investor **from the tree crown to the roots of the tree**.

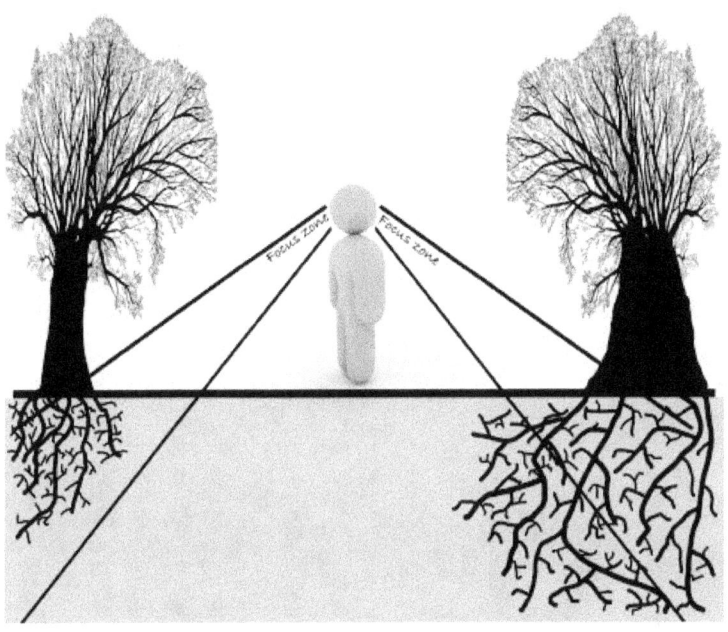

The values are usually hidden, just as you can not see the roots of the trees. As I mentioned before in difficult economic situations people are looking for stability. When people are looking for stability their focuses are changing. They are not looking anymore at the fancy tree-bush, not even at the tree trunk but at the roots. HNWI investors will try to make their decisions based on the roots of the tree.

Every wealth manager knows that if their company is not able to generate profit then it will not survive for a long time. But fewer wealth manager understands that if they can not create value for their clients then they have no future at all.

So closing this example, **the key to prosper is to focus on the values**. To present our knowledge, heritage and uniqueness to our prospective and current clients. When the clients understand our values and they can relate to them as well, then your business will prosper in long term.

Targeting you competitors

During the last years I always got the same excuse from my Clients: "we are in Crisis". Based on my own opinion it is the "easy way" to explain the underperformance. No matter that we are not in 2008-2009 anymore it is always among the top excuses.

I was always forced by life to find solutions and I believe I mastered the Chinese meaning of the word "Crisis". For me Crisis equals with opportunity therefore I created a strategical example to explain my point of view. Since many years now this example is one of the most feared strategy of mine and my favourite one as well because it is so simple, but it also **requires courage to execute it** well.

Believe it or not **most of your prospective clients are already right in front of you**. Let me explain it for you for the perspective of a local wealth management service provider in Monaco. I always say that the prospective clients are already in The Principality of Monaco and most of them ready to be your client.

You can do the same old methods hoping to survive or you can take the opportunity and challenge your market. So let me show you just one simple thing why Crisis is your best friend to improve and to gain new prospective clients.

Let's say that we have five buildings representing your company and other four of your competitors in The Principality of Monaco. All the buildings are different in size and width.

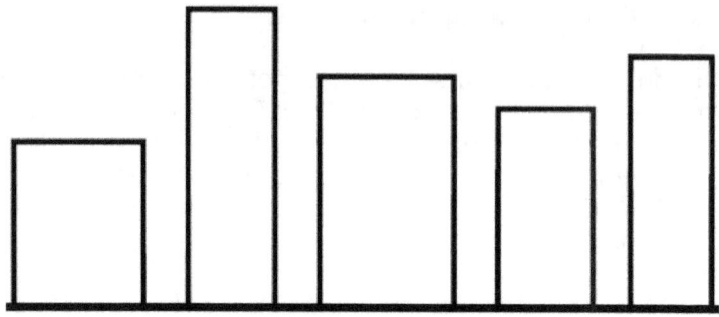

So it is your business and your competitors. Most of the companies are fighting for new clients during ideal business climates. **There are always new clients no matter how is the economic climate is.** There are not so many new clients during bad economic periods but you can still always find some.

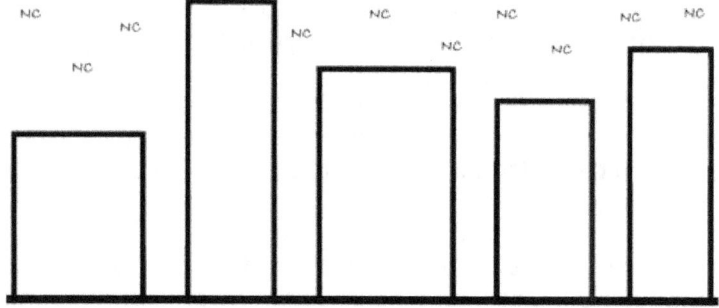

Let's say that the combination of the "NC" letters around the buildings, standing for the New Clients. The biggest problem is that it is very hard to target the new clients in changing economic situations.

When the economic situation is changing, let's say you are facing an after effect of a crisis, corporates start to cut back their marketing budget. They are doing this because they realise the truth that targeting those new clients is becoming very tricky and often ineffective. Therefore budget cutting makes sense for them. However this is exactly why you are struggling.

They are hoping to survive just as all the companies who are following this strategy. However **relying only on hope makes a very weak chance for you**. Let me tell you why.

When companies are cutting back their marketing budget they act according to the Law of attraction. They will start to loose clients. This means you are influenced by the crisis and you are just going with the flow.

Let's put it in this way. In crisis you are loosing clients, which forces your company to cut back the budget to avoid further instability.

The problem with instability is that your whole environment feels it. Not to mention that companies who lost clients between fifteen or twenty percent can be very insecure or even they can go bankrupt. And what does this mean?

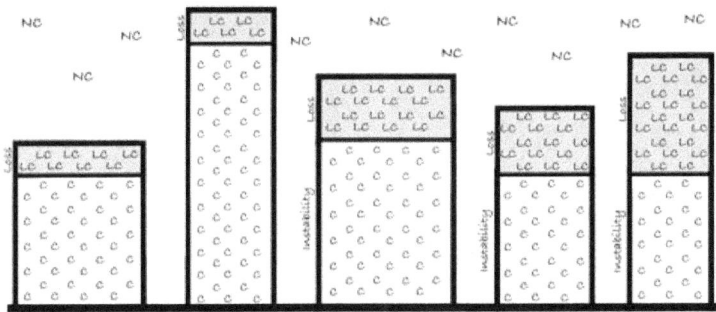

Let's draw the twenty percent margin lines, as well as the "LC" signs, which stood for the Lost Clients and under the margin line the "C" signs, which represents the existing Clients.

These are the twenty percent lines where the instability starts. Of course this can be more or less depending on the size and the reserve of the company.

As you can see there are plenty of Lost Clients in the twenty percent margin. We usually never target them, because it requires too much effort to get them under our umbrella. Not to mention that many of the lost clients have no more funds to restart properly or even if they have they will cause much more extra work.

They seems as free clients on the market **but** actually **they are lost clients** on the market and **this is a huge difference**. Most of them are without further trust and probably without the necessary amount to restart.

In crisis or in any bad economic situation the solution is to target the Clients who stayed with your competitors, the "C"-s.

So let's draw a little "P" letter in front of all the "C"-s so we get the combination of letters "PC", which represent now the Prospective Clients.

In crisis people are looking for different values than before. Price and marketing blah-blah are becoming a lower priority. In these times the **clients are looking for stability, trust and long term solutions**. Therefore the market needs are changing and you can not serve this new market needs if you are just one of the 90 banks and wealth managers.

If you target your new clients in the same old way, you will realise that you are doing the same old strategy and you will receive much less result. And this is only your fault because you let yourself being effected by the outside factors without thinking outside the box and challenging the existing potentials.

You have to think about to **target all the clients who already invested into your competitors**. I would **offer them the same product for the same price or even higher**. Yes, higher. And why the hell would they change to us for a higher price?

Because in crisis clients seek stability in the first place. Price becomes the third or much lower priority. If you are able to **offer stability, security** and you can **gain their trust** then you have a whole new market. And believe it or not they will be happy to change companies if you can convince them regarding the security and the added values from your side. This is why smart companies are able to grow even ten times more than any others during troubled economic times. **Crisis always brings a new market.**

Thinking outside the box. **Amateurs are trying to push and force their corporate messages meanwhile professionals are realising the market gap**, selecting the prospective clients and targeting them. If you are going with the average you will receive the same result than the average. However if you are ready to challenge the existing economic situations then you have the possibility to grow.

In crisis you never cut back your marketing budget because it is your tool to communicate with the prospective clients. You just reorganise your focus and you definitely send out the message that you are not effected by the crisis, you are there and your stability is hard as a rock.

And as I mentioned in the beginning of the chapter **this strategy requires courage**. You have to be confident in your message and communication as well as you need to see your competitors as a business opportunity.

Sadly the Principality of Monaco is a very small and concentrated territory where among the local specialities you can find common activities as well. This means for example that many companies are playing football together therefore lot of managers are afraid to hurt their competitors because it would fragile the friendship.

I believe **business and friendship are two very different things**. When you are in a need to develop your business then you have to grab your opportunities and you have to capitalise all the potentials of your market. Do not forget that sometimes the easiest way is to target your competitors and to show their clients your strengths and added values.

Chapter 06
The Trick

The three basic ingredients

Have you every thought about how do successful people achieve their aims in the same economic environment? Have you every struggled with your performance while having a deep desire to more forward with your aims? Would you like to turn this around?

I have struggled a lot in my life to find the proper ways to **break down the obstacles and to find the breakthrough**. My road was a learning cycle and I realised that revenue increasing refers to the excuse handling and the sales closing. The aim is to get your message out, generate interest, handle the questions and excuses and finally close that deal.

The **three basic ingredients** of successful selling in any business are:

> ➡ Enthusiasm,

> ➡ Belief and

> ➡ Understanding.

The first two, Enthusiasm and Belief are quite obvious. You have to be enthusiastic because that is the most powerful way to deliver the passion and energies. You also have to believe in the product or service you sell otherwise your prospective buyer will feel your insecurity.

Therefore the most effective sales people who know their products, they love them and they are able to transform this sufficient amount of energy into the mind of the prospect.

But the **secret ingredient** is the third one, **Understanding**.

I know many business people aiming to achieve their aims, who are going to various events, "networking", spending huge amounts for different business lunches and dinners, and they are 100% confident that if they are networking more and meeting with much more people then based on the quantity they will have more businesses at the end of the day.

This is what is not working anymore. What they do not realize is that they are continuously spreading the message about their products and trying to sell to everyone. They forget the most important thing, which is to **understand what the prospective clients really want**.

When you are selling you should **never push your message** onto someone because that will automatically create **resistance**.

I want to ask you one question which will dramatically increase your results. Ask yourself only one thing:

What is in it for the buyer?

People are always ready to buy when you are able to deliver something useful for them. This means they can **improve quality, gain** more **time** or **efficiency**, or they can **increase** their **income**.

The most important thing is that you have to see the deal from the perspective of the buyer. You have to understand how he can capitalize your product to gain at least one of the previously mentioned benefits.

When your clients understand how they can improve quality, gain more time or efficiency, or increase income by using your service or product, then they will be ready to close that deal.

Personally I always start my negotiations with this question: What is in it for the buyer?

When your mind is focused and you are able to answer to this question then you will be ready to convince the prospective buyer. This is one of my best suggestion for you to think about this before your sales meetings:

What is in it for the buyer?

Educate your target group

As I mentioned it before it is very important to remember that everyone can see the price of the product but not its value! **We need to show and teach the value of the product in all cases.**

You can have the best product ever, or you can provide the most professional services but they will not matter in the eye of your prospective clients. The customers do not really care about the product itself. The most **important challenge** for you and your business is to show and teach the customers **how can they use it and make benefits** from your product or solution. This will be the main decision points of the prospective clients.

Client education is one of the most important task of a company. If you are not able to teach the values of your product you will not be different from your competitors. And when you are unable to offer a different product or solution then the prospective clients will **automatically compare you**. This will be the point when your one and only competitive advantage will be the price of the product. This is the point when you can start to close your business.

The more comparable you are, the more boring you are in your market. Even if you are selling the same product as many of your competitors you can still educate the customer in various ways.

If you are selling shaving sets then teach the customers how to shave stylish beards, when you are selling wallpapers show them how can they create amazing and individual interiors for their own personality. If you are a wine distributor do a food and wine culinary recipe series. **You do not need to**

change your product, but you have to show the difference by teaching the value of your product.

The more interesting is your education message the more viral will it be and this will bring you new audience as well. Remember that the very first key is to send out the message. When you found an interesting way to speak to your prospective clients then you will position your company very high.

Teach your value because it will take you out from the competition to a whole new level.

Five reasons why people do not buy from you (online)

Online sales, online stores and automatized marketing is all around us. It is almost impossible to find a website today which is not aiming at selling something. But are they really successful?

Sending out your message is one thing and to get an exchange from it in the form of money is another thing. There can be many reasons for not buying, which can be different for each individual.

Herewith I will disclose you the "secret 5" of online income. Five things which will boost your online selling.

The number one is clear communication. **One of the basic reason why people immediately turn down an offer is because they do not understand it's message.** Your communications should be always very clear, easy to understand and to the point.

People do not have time to read tens of pages talking about something what you can explain in two sentences as well. Create **short and clear communications which highlight the substance**.

The **second reason for refusal is when people do not see the value** in your service or product. This is what I call the "what is in it for him?" part. It is of key importance to explain well how the prospect can utilize your offer to gain more profit, time or quality in his own field of activity.

When people can not see value in your offer you have no more chance to succeed. Consider the explanation of the value as your major weapon to sell.

When we are talking about sales-pitch descriptions and explanations here comes the third challenge. **People need to believe in it** or like what you offer. Therefore **you need to communicate in the same level as your target group needs and understands**.

When you make a clear communication, the explanation of the value and you are able to trigger the belief in the prospective buyers towards your offer then you have almost succeeded.

Once you have gone through all the reasons above, you can get to the point where people do not buy now, which is the hardest obstacle because it seems there is no logical reasoning behind it. In most cases you will face two obstacles.

The obstacle number four is when the **prospect can not afford it**. No mater how good your product is if the prospect has not enough money to buy. When you are selling for a major company then this is not an issue, however many small businesses, private persons are very sensitive for their budget.

The solution for this problem could be to reduce their initial payment into multiple forms to buy. When you are able to find suitable financial solutions then you will overcome this obstacle.

Finally the last obstacle which is considered as a major suffering point for most sales people is that **the buyers don't want it now**.

Even if people feel and know that they need your product or solution, **99% of the people go into a hidden denial** when you want to implement some changes around them.

Often they are ready to postpone the decision which is a major problem for you because with the time passing they can easily loose their intent in your product.

To overcome this obstacle you need to offer something which gives the buyer an **extra advantage to buy**.

For example when you sell a product you can create a promotional action which ends this week. Or you can offer an added value when the prospect signs the deal this week. For example when you sell cars you can offer a set of summer tires to motivate the prospect to a quick decision.

Even if you do not sell products you can offer **added values** for a solution as well. For example if you sell business consulting you can ensure two days of free implementation training besides the service the prospect is aiming to buy.

The key is to ensure the added value as a **time sensitive offer**. This way the buyer will understand that during this period he gets more exchange for his money. When you have no other obstacles then this could be a major motivation to close the deal.

Summarizing everything, the secret Five of the online income is:

➡ clear communication

➡ explaining the value

➡ make people believe in it (or like it)

➡ suitable financial possibilities

➡ time sensitivity

Appropriate communication

Speaking properly to your target group in the way they really understands it, writing the right marketing message is one of the most difficult step during the marketing planning campaigns.

One of the most important thing when writing the marketing text is to try to describe the same thing as if we would be discussing it personally. If this is done then it just has to be combined and you are ready for the advertisement.

It is very important that we dare to write why the product or service is good for the target people, and what they need to do to make the products or services theirs. You should not be afraid to ask from the clients/customers or even to give instructions to them.

If your clients are contacted through the Internet or direct mail marketing campaign, the so-called Borden's formula can be a very useful thing. This comes from Richard C. Borden, head of New York University. He used this formula to originally make his classes more exciting, but it is perfect for attracting attention in offers, advertisements, letters.

The formula includes 4 simple steps:

1., "Who cares...."
Say something that will make the other look up, that will erase the other's indifference or carelessness and will make them immediately look up at you, will take you into consideration.

2., "Why am I talking about this"
Explain why it is important for the OTHER, why you want to talk or write to him or her. After this, tell your "story" very shortly, aiming to the point.

3., "For example...."
Tell the Other person one or more real life examples that illustrate and make your point more realistic.

4., "So what?"
Help the other Person get to the conclusion that you want him or her to get: why is it good, important for him or her, etc. if he or she does what you are asking him or her.

The Borden formula is a very efficient method, but you should never forget that writing marketing and advertisement texts is a separate profession. There are still lots of other tricks and methods, with which you can continuously develop your base of knowledge.

The only important thing in marketing campaigns, promotional materials and marketing texts is that they communicate. They should be personal and should communicate that they are a great opportunity for the person who is reading them and that they have been written exactly for him or her.

Using formulas in the business life

The previously presented Borden formula is a great tool to understand the right and appropriate communication towards our target group. However in many cases we need to find our own way to communicate. There are business segments, industries where you can not use the Borden formula in the efficiency you desire. Therefore you need to challenge it in a way it serve you the best.

Let's see some other examples how can you attract people with your communication message in different ways.

AIDA formula

Attention - Interest - Desire - Action

Attention
Say something that will attract your reader's attention

Interest
Tell the other person why he or she should be interested in the issue and why he or she should believe what you are saying.Prove that what you are saying is true and real (case studies, offerings, opinions, references, etc.)

Desire
Write down, list your product's or services' advantages, effects on the other person's life, business etc. You should achieve that the other person should WANT, desire your Product, service or You as a professional, what you are offering.

Action
Tell the other person to react to your offer if the interest has been lighten up and tell him or her to do it now.

Best practices for Offer writing

Desire - Problem - Fears - Solution - Advantages - References

Desire
Write down what you want to sell

Problem
Describe why it would be necessary for the other person to buy it, to take what you are offering.

Fears
You need to list here the excuses that clients might say

Solution
Repeat in 2-3 lines the solution. You mention the price here!

Advantages
What is the advantage by buying your product or service

References
Client or reference opinion, reference

CV formula

Desire - Problem - Fears - Solution - Advantages - References

Desire
I want to have a position as a project manager in your company.

Problem
This would be good for you because...with my experiences....I can add to your success in this way.....

Fears
Many companies do not take, consider applicants over 40 years old. They forget that between 20 and 30 years old people change their jobs more often, while a person more mature is much more loyal to their jobs, positions and consider their tasks, jobs as part of their whole life.

Solution
The expertise and experience is priceless.

Advantage
I am not a simple expert, professional, your company forms part of my Life...

References
Reference from who you know, who knows you as well.

The weakness of the advertisement

One of my very favourite segment for waste of money is the advertisement business. I see so many company owners pushing incredible amounts of advertisements which are never getting back to them the requested results.

Of course media agencies are alway ready to print out all the appearances and place tens of folders with various advertisements. It is nice indeed, but is it really considered as profit?

No. Not a problem at all. Many of the business owners have the same self justification, when they say: "Maybe we did not grew as we expected with this campaign, but at least we strengthen our brand name in the market."

It sounds correct isn't it? Except the fact that wasting money does not help at all to the growth potential. If you target do it well.

The biggest problem with the advertisement that most of them are not communicating directly to the client. And even if they do, they do not really giving the chance to create two way communication.

In life and business one of the most important thing is communication. Communication should be two ways every time. I consider all marketing campaign useless and wasteful where there are not two ways communication with the prospective clients. Let's look at this a little in details.

Most of the company leaders are afraid from the PR and marketing areas because they have had bad experiences. In the last ten years most of the companies just bought advertisements and never generated big results. Of course: bad market, crisis, the weather, etc... there are many excuses.

In 2008 I consulted a company where the CEO spent lots of money for various television, radio, and printed campaigns.

I asked him, the company CEO, what the result was? He said some generation of new sales.

I asked him whether he was satisfied? He said no...

I asked him what he thought the problem was? He said the problem might be with the product because the PR company made a lot of beautiful advertisements and they presented 7 folders full with press releases.

I was really shocked because he let himself believe that the problems was his own product. So I had no other choice and I pointed to him that his own mind was the problem...

The PR is not about press releases! This is the same case in marketing just as it is in PR.

If your promotion, campaign does not create, generate reactions then you throw your money out of the window.

RULE: The main task of the PR is to generate reaction! Not articles, press releases, REACTION!

Today the companies measure the PR values by Kilograms... The PR companies fills up 5-10 folders with press releases and advertisements... Who cares about the results? Who cares about the revenues? Only

YOU!!!! When you started the co-operation with the PR company you wanted more incoming money, not more costs for yourself... If we see the result from this point, from your owner point of view, then you can ask whether the 10 folders give you any result? No.

We use the communication verbal or written, because we want reactions. If there were no reactions then it was just a wasted time. The main task of the communication is to send a message to people and to get back a reaction or an answer.

Most of the marketing companies always break this rule. I always see campaigns like this: "Buy Lemonade!" Ok, thanks maybe next time. Never tell the client what he/sheI really wants... Never push you company message and force someone to do something. Always go back to the old rule: What is in it for the buyer?

Now-days many media agencies are trying to sell advertisement places for you, meanwhile PR agencies are pushing their brand promotion, brand development services. They are always ready to charge their hourly fees sky high, but my number one rule is for promotions is:

Never trust in a company who is working just for fix amounts.

Never. If they work for fix amounts they are not motivated and 99% of times they just want your money. If you can create (maybe with a good help) a two way communication channel with your clients, possible buyers you will be much more efficient!

Before I would go any further there is another thing which is often faded away, which is the education of the value. PR means that you have to make known a product/solution in a wider group, and you have to create a good opinion about that product/solution. This is almost impossible if you are forcing your brand instead of the value of your product or service.

You can not generate selling if people do not know your product or if they have a bad opinion about your product. How many sales people can sell a very bad quality, unnamed product? Not so many...

When marketing people says that the economic is bad, or the market is not ready for a product that only means that they were unable to find the way to teach the value of the product to the appropriate target group.

People are always ready to buy! The only mistake you made was that your PR was not good, in all other cases you can make revenue easily. If you or your consultant partner can create a good opinion about your product/ solution and can make it known in wider areas, then you can sell in a much easier way.

Let me share with you a basic trick for selling.

Many years ago I was a lucky owner of a Range Rover Sport, a Land Rover Defender 60th Anniversary Limited Edition and a Lotus Elise 40th Anniversary Limited Edition. Buying these cars I get into a very good relationship with the CEO and the owner of the Land Rover distributor group.

One day we talked about the European auto market and the strategies they use to target the customers. Without revealing big secrets I can tell that they are put enormous efforts to get a clients.

Buying a luxury car is not the same as buying a croissant next to our morning coffee. I got to know that in this industry very often there is two-three years between the first contact and the actual buying.

Many people are very careful with a decision where they place thousands of Euros and because of this the ask for flyers, they go to test drive, the go to another test drive, etc... and during this time the dealer has a huge responsibility to keep up the interest and also to keep the prospective client, do not let him go to the competitor dealer.

Probably this was the point when I realised and understood why I do not like the standard media approach.

Imagine that you have a media campaign in a magazine which is capable to reach out thirty-five thousand people. Let's say five thousand people will actually read your advertisement from this audience. From the five thousand maybe hundred will be interested in your offer.

Most of the companies would be very satisfied with this result since their campaign delivered new clients for them. Getting new clients helps us to survive in the market and this is very important. However the real deal is when you are able to capitalise most of your potential. And in this case the two new clients are not your full potential.

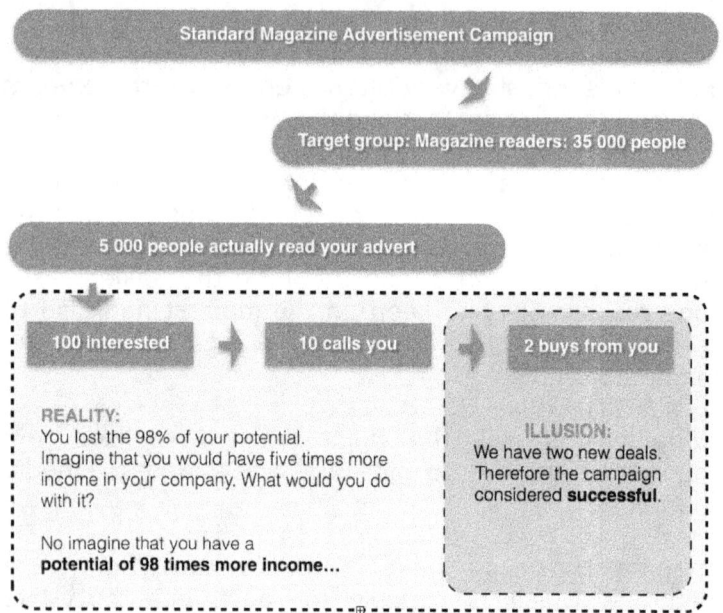

As you can see one of the major problem with this type of approach that it does not motivate the client for reaction or iteration with you. And without direct communication lines no matter how good is your offer you simply can not convince them to buy from you.

However your true potential is the one-hundred people who actually interested in your product or service. Therefore your marketing campaign should focus on them as well and it should ensure the possibility for you to convince them.

So back to my life... In those times when I realised the Land Rover marketing approach problem I was happily married and my wife had a very interesting habit. She was passionate for shoes (just as most of the women), however she never could made her shoe choice or make her decision immediately on spot in the store. Inside in her soul she knew that she like that specific shoe, when she tried it it was perfect in her leg, but still she always went further with the hope to find something better.

Then I realised that she is not looking for better. She already knew that the previous one was the right one, however she was afraid to commit herself. Many of us are afraid to make our choices therefore we are "shopping" around. It is very rare when someone immediately buys the very first product he or she sees without even compare it with an alternative one.

People are like to "shop around", people like to compare. Therefore many time they see more alternative before they make their decision. Statistically proven that an average customer compares at least seven different product or service before he/she makes his/her final decision.

The big question is always the same. **Can you be the one who close the deal or not?**

If you can not close the majority of the deals then you have a huge loss on the potentials. In a long term business model it is never enough to survive. All businesses need to focus on prosperity.

In many businesses we have to face with the harsh reality that we spend weeks with the client, we educated him and suddenly he buy it from our competitors. To avoid this type of negative experiences and basically waste of time, money, energy and efforts we need to control the prospective buyers from the very beginning. For this the very first step is to get their contact immediately at the first interaction point.

Opt-In structure

The very first key towards any kind of prospective client iteration is to get his/her direct contact. The challenge is that people do not really like to give this information out. To convince them to trust you you need to forget your old Internet approach model and you have to build up a new strategy based on a value-sequence.

The very first thing is that you need to separate your website into (at least) three different and separate site.

- ➡ Your company homepage
- ➡ Your value page
- ➡ Your sales page

Your homepage will be your professional introduction page. It will be a surface where you can communicate your company informations, news and the basic details of your products/services. It can be a big and detailed collection of various and relevant information.

However because most of the company home pages are containing way more information therefore the values are usually hidden. To solve this we have to set up very clean Value pages.

The main aim of the Opt-In structure that you offer something which will teach your prospect or which will handle his/her fear. Something which is really valuable for him/her. Just value, nothing for sale.

The value page usually focuses only on one single customer problem or solution. It is very clean and all it is promising is the solution for free. This is very important because this will be the carrot which will motive the prospect to give you its contact details.

Obviously our aim is to sell, therefore we have to build up a sales strategy on our Opt-In surface. Even the easiest strategies are built up on the following three pillars.

➡ Add value

➡ Educate the lead

➡ Sell something

Value page

On the Value page you have to focus on a key message which usually handles the fear of the prospective client. You need to find a topic which will help him to find solution for his biggest concern regarding your product.

You have to grab his attention immediately (such as in the Borden formula) therefore we usually use four sections.

➡ Tagline

➡ Headline

➡ Video (optional)

➡ Body

In the TAGLINE it is very important to have a little bit of negative approach because people usually more committed for this kind of communication.

Some examples:

➡ Real-Estate: The biggest real-estate problems!

➡ Wealth Management: What is the reason why wealth managers fails to protect your wealth?

➡ Snow tires: Why people die with snow tires?

➡ Insurance: Cases where your insurance will not pay!

➡ Art: The reason why people will not buy from You!

When our tagline is negative enough we will grab the attention of the prospective client, so we can focus on the development of the fear in the HEADLINE.

The HEADLINE is usually a short statement why is it important for the Prospect to listen to you message.

After the headline we can include a BODY part as well, where we can ensure the prospect that we are here to let his fear gone, therefore we offer him more and more information to handle his fears. all he needs to do is to register and we immediately send him the document which will made him more relieved.

TAGLINE **The biggest real-estate problem in Monaco!**

HEADLINE
Do NOT rent or buy before you read this! The 10 key factors to Protect your investment.

VIDEO MESSAGE

BODY
Get your FREE case-study of "Real-Estate in Monaco" by entering your name and e-mail below.

Name:

E-mail:

Many times it is also recommended to use a small video which starts automatically when someone opens the value page. It is very important that in this video our intention to add value or teach something which can generate benefit of the visitor.

It can not be a company introduction or a product description it should be something which teach or educate values. For example if you selling hair styling gel, de not talk about the product but show 5 cool and trendy ways to change your look. This will create the value and this will grab the attention of the prospective client.

If you approach is strong enough then you will motivate the prospect to register for the next material and this is when you can start your targeting by your sequence page.

Sequence page

The sequence page is the page where you fulfil your promise and you deliver the content you offered in exchange for the registration. It should have an automatic and immediate process. The best way if the prospective client receives this material no less than five minutes after the registration.

This will build up the confidence in the prospective client that you are the man of your words and he did well to trust in you.

Very important that we promised a content that is valuable, therefore do not push sales messages to the prospect because that will automatically create resistance. You promised value, so give value and just value.

Since now you have the name and the direct e-mail address of your prospect you can build up a sequence where you can give more value. For example after three days you can send on more material just to give him more information about the topic.

Another five days later you can send him a much valuable material which is still free for him and which also add value for the prospective client.

The most important that you can do this without any effort. Many internet programs support the automatised sequence based e-mails therefore you have to build up your sequence only one.

When you already offered three-five valuable content then it will be your time to place your own offer to the prospective client.

"We hope you enjoyed our videos and materials so far... If you liked it then you will love this service as well..."

By this time he will know you and understand you better and you will have a better affinity to convince the prospect to buy.

And what if the prospect will not buy? It is not a problem, because you will have the direct contact to approach him/her any time with your future offers.

Real-Estate vs. Wealth Management strategy

There is a problem to solve: Your business field is extremely small and concentrated, therefore to get a business leverage you have to be in charge for the communication and you need to control the approach. You need direct contacts.

In February 2013 me and my friend created one sample strategy for the local bank and wealth manager Barclays in the Principality of Monaco. Since then I got no feed-back and I always had this feeling that it probably ended deep inside a shelf without even gave a chance for it. As many big corporation all around the World Barclays had a headquarter too and as I got to know later they have a very strict global marketing strategy. Too bad...

However I am not surprised because to capitalise it you need to understand the local needs which you simply can not adapt sitting in a foreign country. It is also a strategy where you have to be very open minded and you have to think out of the box.

So back in February 2013 I provided to Barclays a sample solution, which could have bring it many new clients in 2013 and it had the possibility as well to bring less stress to the employees and the management team. So this is what I wrote to them...

All my ideas are focusing on actual **new clients, more free time** for new developments and **budget saving** as it will be clearly seen at the end of this concept sample.

I already collected more than 75 ways to increase Barclays' client numbers and from these 10 are ways for Barclays to tackle its real estate issue. In the following concept sample I would like to share with Barclays one of them. There are many ways Barclays would never have thought of but I want to give now a concrete example.

Barclays is paying too much marketing/promotional/ event/advertisement/referral fee for the real estate agents, which is a big part of its budget, for new clients. So this is how I would describe it:

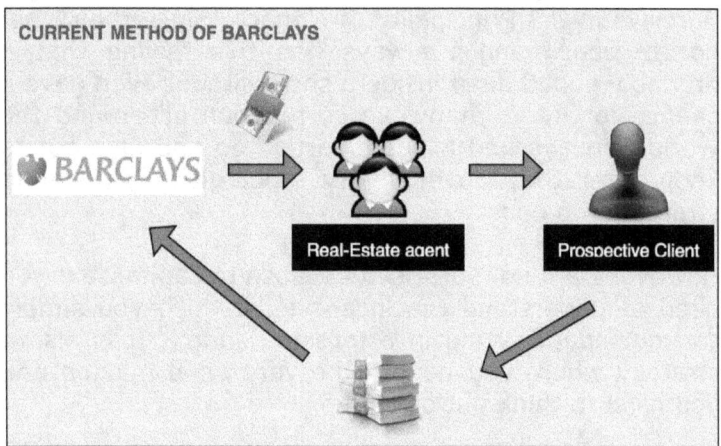

So, as it can be seen Barclays is paying for the real estate agents to introduce it to some of their clients.

However I see three issues:

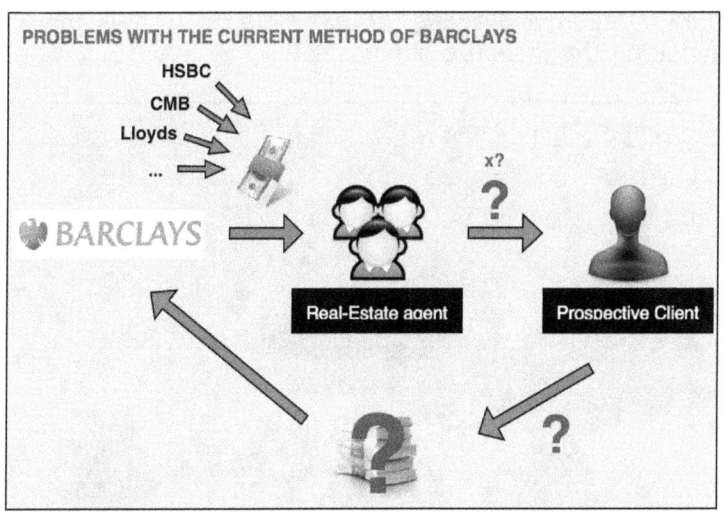

PROBLEMS WITH THE CURRENT METHOD OF BARCLAYS

1. Barclays does not know actually the number of clients the real estate agents really introduce Barclays to.

2. Barclays does not know wether the real estate agent is accepting money from other banks as well or not.

3. Since Barclays does not have direct contact with the prospective client, it has no control over what is communicated to them about Barclays specifically.

The exchange is probably not in balance with the results.

Let's imagine what would happen if I would offer Barclays a full contact list of all the new residents and investors in real estate. This would be a real powerful list.

And let's imagine that this list includes all Barclays' competitors' clients as well. Here it's important to remember my drawing of example with five blocks including the insecure clients...

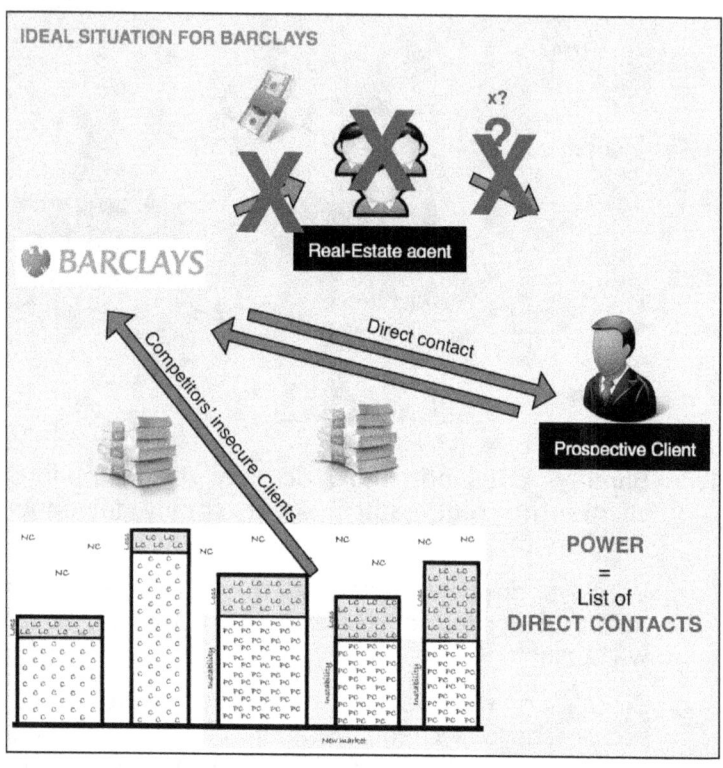

Wouldn't it be a huge asset, since these are all direct contacts? Can we reach this with any kind of event or advertisement?

We can reach this in many ways, I drafted 10 different ways for this.

One of the way is this: handling the fear of people.

This should be parallel with the existing process with the real estate agents. Barclays will see in 6 months how it will change everything, by which time it will not need the agents as intermediaries anymore.

Every person who invests high amounts has one common feature, which is **fear of making a bad, wrong decision**. And in many cases they question any consultant, agent because they know they are advising for a profit and not for their best interest.

Let's imagine that Barclays would have a Magic Pill for the fear of these people who are ready to invest high amounts, in this case in real estate in Monaco.

BARCLAYS = MAGIC PILL

for handling FEAR

for giving VALUE

for building TRUST

With such a Magic Pill let's imagine Barclays could build up trust, professionalism, security, long-term commitment and possible clients because of all these reasons.

Step 1: Why will people interact with Barclays?

Let's create a short pdf file, which focuses on the important things related to investing in real estate in Monaco. We could title this from the point of view of the FEAR of the Prospects, for example:

"13 things before you invest in Monaco"

OR

"**Don't buy** property in Monaco **before you read this**"

The important thing is to grab the **attention** with the **title** by handling the fear of the people.

We could call this material as a **short case study** and add a **value** to it. For example 1500 Euro.

To add value to it is very important because this will give it seriousness and further value.

Step 2: Get the direct contact

Let's get the contacts.

We have to be realistic, of course nobody will pay for this material and this is not our aim either because we are not a publisher.

It is human that people do not like things that are free. However if something is very valuable like 1500 Euro they would like to get it for free. Let's imagine that we are giving Louis Vuitton bags for free.

So if we can create something, which is valuable and which handles people's fear they will want to get it for free.

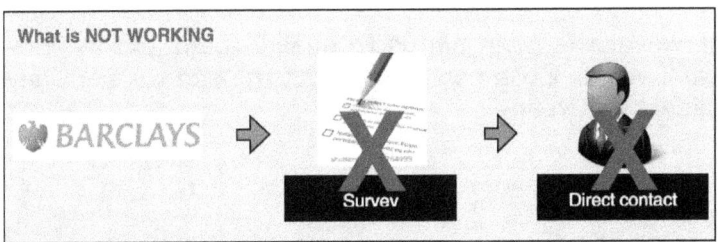

However we have to be aware that what does not work is if we push our prospect to fill out a long survey. I also hate to fill out forms with 3-5 questions.

Prospects want trust and value first and foremost.

What works is to ask only a name and an email for which in exchange to offer to send them this case study for the value of 1500 Euro.

This way they will receive something useful, which is of value for them and builds up trust and we will have an unqualified contact list, which is already good for Barclays newsletters, advertisements, PR campaign, etc.

At this point we will have a huge list with unfiltered prospective clients.

However the main aim is to qualify them and to know who we can close now because at the end we want new clients this year.

Step 3: Qualify the prospects

In this following step our aim is to qualify and filter the contacts, those who are serious versus unserious, based on their assets, intents (now, future or past), etc.

To get these further, detailed and mostly private information we have to make the prospect fill out a survey. Even if there is already a form of trust because of our gift it is still a hard work to get these information.

So we have to use the same solution, which has already worked. We will create another PDF file, a much more detailed one. We have to provide issues to the prospect, keeping in mind handling his fear, which hold key importance for them. Such as:

➡ real-estate trends in Monaco

➡ developments of the districts of Monaco, the future Golden Square

➡ where to invest in short, medium and long term

➡ analysis of the investment returns

➡ steps to become a resident of Monaco

If we can collect these information into a PDF we can call it again a Barclays Case Study. And since it is a much detailed collection of knowledge we can value it for 8000 Euro.

So following some weeks of our original gif we can offer this additional case study to the registered prospects. However at this point we can say that it is not for free. In exchange for the 8000 Euro detailed

Barclays Case Study we will ask the Prospect to answer 10 questions which are valuable for Barclays. (Such as asset, time, contact details, etc...)

At this point all the unserious people will skip the registration, however the real prospects will be ready to fill it out because we have already formed some kind of trust by ensuring the first material.

They will be our Filtered contacts and we will have valuable information to close them, they will be our real prospects to close with direct channels.

This is just one simple way to collect prospective clients, but this way Barclays will have direct contact information, valuable data regarding the intent and the assets and continuous possibility to grow and to target new people.

Even after the first registration Barclays can target them with various offers. They are direct contacts, which cannot be achieved with a marketing advertisement that maybe never reaches them.

Not to mention that Barclays will pay every time for the different marketing advertisements, meanwhile these contacts will be there for Barclays forever without spending any extra amount to approach them.

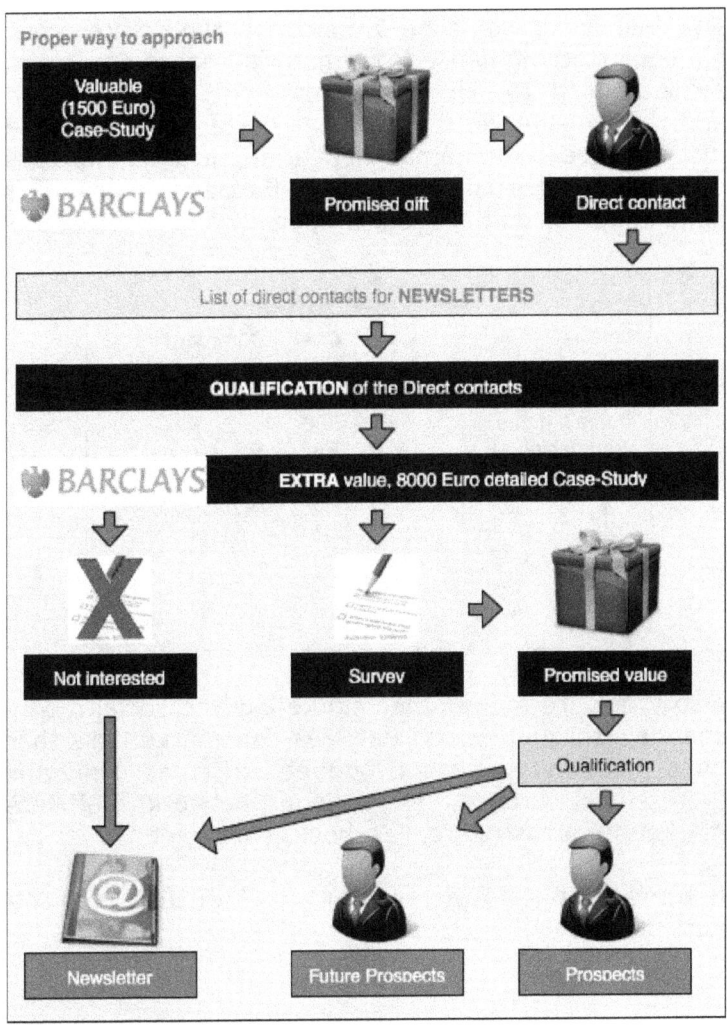

The cost of all would be 0, since we can create the 2 pdf case study in house from material that is public and available from the Monaco Government. For the design and the website we can create a barter with someone just to have their names appearing, just as Barclays did with its Greek partners. Also, Barclays can run this page under its domain as a subpage.

COST CALCULATION

Item	Cost	Comment
Teaser case-study	0 Euro	*In-house*
Full case-study	0 Euro	*In-house+Barter*
Domain name	9 Euro*	
Web design	0 Euro	*Barter (logo)*
Web programming	0 Euro	*Barter (logo)*
Hosting and maintenance	0 Euro	*Barter (logo)*
Total:	**9 Euro***	

*Or **0 Euro** if you use subdomain, such as XYZ.barclays.com

Also there are many other marketing and social media channels through which Barclays can market this that does not involve extra budget, such as LinkedIN Professional Groups, Professional networks, affiliate marketing, newsletters, Facebook, twitter, etc.

I have not enough paper to mention all the possibilities.

The reverse side

Obviously it was very hard for me to understand the lack of intentions for changing and opening up for new business channels, but I knew that I am unable to change the global strategy of a corporate board. Especially not since they sat thousands of kilometres away from Monaco.

So it was time to move on, even if I really liked this strategy. I believe it is a powerful approach where you do not push your message, but you ensure valuable information and knowledge. Not to mention that this strategy works in its reverse way as well.

If you have a real-estate agency you can use the Barclays strategy in for your own benefits. You just have to think about the most important topics, issues and needs what your clients will facing. I would definitely create information approach for the previous example topics:

- ➡ real-estate trends in Monaco
- ➡ developments of the districts of Monaco, the future Golden Square
- ➡ where to invest in short, medium and long term
- ➡ analysis of the investment returns
- ➡ steps to become a resident of Monaco

And I would also approach the prospective clients in a personal way as well:

- schools and education in Monaco
- relocating Monaco
- living with a baby in Monaco
- how can you have a job in Monaco

Furthermore I would also benefit from the power of the administration requirements:

- VISA permits
- residence permit (carte de sejour)
- marriage in Monaco
- heritage protection
- taxation rules

Etc...

There are so many options to grab the attention of the prospective clients. You should never gave out valuable information without any exchange therefore when you can find a topic which is really interest for your target group you have to build up an opt-in structure on it. This way you will have a fair exchange which will be the direct contact to the prospective clients.

Do not forget as soon you have the direct contact of the prospect you can start to educate him, put him on the newsletter and other communications and you will be able to for him to a client of yours.

The opt-in strategy is much more cost effective than any other media advertisement and since it brings immediate value to the prospects they will spread the word about is. And once the word of mouth started you will see the growing of your potentials.

Chapter 07
Final thoughts

In business making money is easy. The difficult is to keep up your positive attitude and to feed your ability to continuously look for the new things. To not to be afraid of change.

The problems will distract your focus every single time. So be it. However you have to have the courage to confront with your monsters and to fight for the solutions.

> *"An excuse is worse than a mistake"*
> - Dodo Newman

In the world of economy there are no such thing as only losers. In every economic situation you can find winners, no matter who hard it effected the other people. These people are not special, they just never gave up on their dreams.

I read one day that most of the people are giving up on their aims just one step before they would reach the breakthrough. It is not something I teach to my clients.

The courage to change and challenge things is in all of us. Just imagine when you were a child and you tried to ride a bike. It did not matter who much you fall, you went back until you finally reached you aim.

As you can see you do not need the courage to start something, but to finish it. Especially when you start to create something different. You might be also labelled as crazy, idiot or odd, but it will be your living proof that you already started to form opinions. And this is the quality of the winners.

Monaco Experts Academy
- written by Zsolt Szemerszky -

In life we all meet with people with a specific reason.

> *"Some people come in our life as blessings. Others come in our life as lessons."* - Mother Teresa

It is our task to find out why and to make it to our benefit. From my point of you if this book gave you at least one valuable thought than I am truly happy for it.

This case I hope you will like my other books as well such as the:

Creating Business Value

or the

NO EXCUSE! in business

And please do not forget what I always used to say:

> *"Every mountain can be climbed*
> *just you have to find the appropriate way to it.*
> *If somebody does not achieve it's goal*
> *then he has not done everything to achieve it.*
> *The secret of success is persistence!"*

Good luck with your business.

Monaco Experts Academy
- written by Zsolt Szemerszky -

Notes

In this book I presented some examples and also mentioned a few company names or individuals.

All of these names and companies are there as sample ones in order to ensure you a better understanding of the contents, examples.

Even if I talked with these people and corporations, maybe consulted them, it does not necessarily true that they used my strategies and thoughts as it is.

This book is more like a Monaco specific business brain storming, than a reference book.

Liability disclaimer

This book/e-book is not a substitute for independent professionals, investment or legal advice.

Present book/e-book is not a case-study or a professional advice. It is an idea starter document to highlight some of the potential areas for improvement of quality and the increase of the number of new clients in various business sectors.

Present book serves as the writer's interpretation of his personal business views, without specific advice on any personal or corporate requirements. Use of any information from this book or any other book or web site referred to is for general information only and does not represent advice either expressed or implied. You are encouraged to seek professional, legal or investment advice.

Accordingly, the author, his publishers and affiliates disclaim that the information provided should not be treated as advice. Furthermore, it is a strict condition of the that any individual reading the book recognizes and accepts unreservedly that all information, analyses, projections, forecasts, expectations, or outcomes relating to past, present, or future financial markets performance, economic activity, or investment or trading instruments, are provided exclusively for academic purposes and that such information must not in any way be construed as general or personal advice to invest or trade in any financial market or security.

The author or publishers shall not be held liable for any losses incurred by anyone who follows or acts on the opinions, views, or forecasts expressed in any form in this e-book, on any other websites or from individuals connected by hyperlink to or from this website. Anyone reading this book is solely responsible for their interpretation of its contents and for their own decisions and actions. The foregoing applies also to correspondence (including private emails), to posts on other websites (including internet message boards and public discussion forums), and to articles published in other mass media.

You should make your own enquiries before entering into any business decision on the basis of the information or material on this e-book. Please ensure you contact an adviser directly to discuss your particular circumstances and how the information provided applies to your situation. Past performance is not indicative of future performance, and involves substantial risks. All readers should consult their own Authorized Business Adviser and/or, Solicitor or other specialists before placing money at risk or attempting to implement any of the strategies discussed, and should always employ prudent policies and practices appropriate to their own particular circumstances.